17182

HOODWINKED

DECEPTION AND RESISTANCE

BY STEPHEN SHAPIRO AND TINA FORRESTER

ART BY DAVID CRAIG

ANNICK PRESS

TORONTO • NEW YORK • VANCOUVER

Edited by Laura Ellis
Book and cover design: Sheryl Shapiro
Image research: Sandra Booth
Photograph credits appear at the back of the book.

Annick Press Ltd.

We acknowledge the support of the Canada Council for the Arts, the Ontario Arts Council, and the Government of Canada through the Book Publishing Industry Development Program (BPIDP) for our publishing activities.

Cataloging in Publication

Shapiro, Stephen, date-
    Hoodwinked : deception and resistance / by Stephen Shapiro and Tina Forrester ; art by David Craig.

(Outwitting the enemy : stories from the Second World War)
Includes index.
ISBN 1-55037-833-3 (bound).—ISBN 1-55037-832-5 (pbk.)

1. World War, 1939-1945—Deception—Juvenile literature.
2. World War, 1939-1945—Underground movements—Juvenile literature.
I. Forrester, Tina II. Craig, David III. Title. IV. Series.

D743.7.S43 2004   j940.54'86   C2003-907419-6

The art in this book was rendered in oils.
The text was typeset in New Baskerville, Serpentine, and Myriad.

Distributed in Canada by:
Firefly Books Ltd.
66 Leek Crescent
Richmond Hill, ON
L4B 1H1

Published in the U.S.A. by Annick Press (U.S.) Ltd.
Distributed in the U.S.A. by:
Firefly Books (U.S.) Inc.
P.O. Box 1338
Ellicott Station
Buffalo, NY 14205

Printed and bound in Belgium.
Visit us at: www.annickpress.com

TIMELINE

1939
Germany invades Poland (September 1)

Britain and France declare war on Germany (September 3)

1940
Germany invades Norway (April 9)

Germany invades France, Belgium, Holland (May 10)

Italy declares war on Allies (June 10)

Battle of Britain begins (August 13)

1941
Germany invades Yugoslavia (April 6)

Germany invades USSR (June 22)

Japan attacks Pearl Harbor (December 7)

1942
Battle of El Alamein, Egypt, begins (October 23)

1943
Warsaw Ghetto Uprising (April 19 – May 16)

Allies invade Sicily (July 10)

Italy surrenders (September 3)

1944
Allies capture Rome (June 4)

D-Day (June 6)

Allies invade southern France (August 15)

1945
President Roosevelt dies (April 12)

Germany surrenders (May 7)

Bombing of Hiroshima (August 6)

Bombing of Nagasaki (August 9)

Japan officially surrenders (September 2)

CONTENTS

An American F4F Wildcat fighter tests its guns

This tank-landing ship could carry 18 heavy tanks or 27 trucks.

Special forces climb an obstacle course at a training camp in England

A WORLD AT WAR

ALLIES:
the alliance during the Second World War that included Great Britain, the United States, Canada, Australia, India, New Zealand, South Africa, the U.S.S.R., China, and many other countries.

AXIS:
the alliance during the Second World War made up of Germany, Italy, Japan, Hungary, Bulgaria, Romania, and Finland.

AXIS OCCUPIED:
Countries occupied by the Axis during the Second World War included France, Belgium, the Netherlands, Denmark, Norway, Poland, Greece, Yugoslavia, the Philippines, and many others.

NEUTRAL:
Countries that remained neutral during the Second World War included Sweden, Switzerland, Portugal, Ireland, Spain, and Turkey.

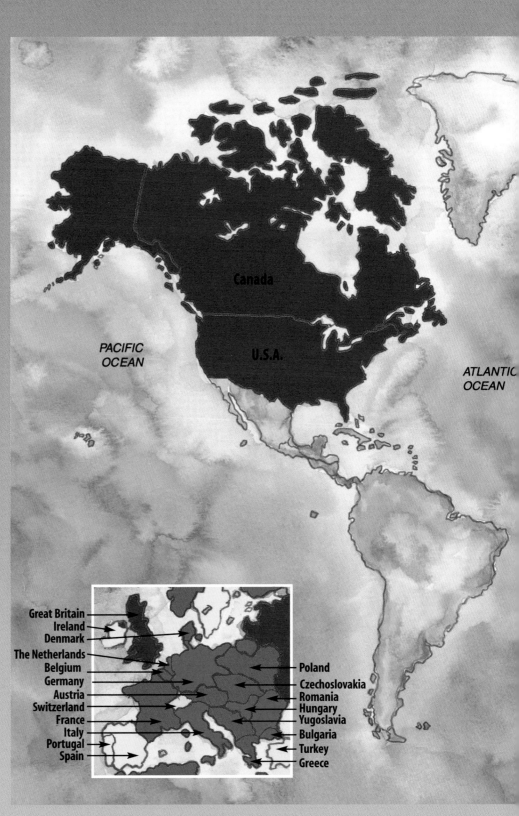

Canada

PACIFIC
OCEAN

U.S.A.

ATLANTIC
OCEAN

Great Britain
Ireland
Denmark
The Netherlands
Belgium
Germany
Austria
Switzerland
France
Italy
Portugal
Spain

Poland
Czechoslovakia
Romania
Hungary
Yugoslavia
Bulgaria
Turkey
Greece

INTRODUCTION

The Second World War happened half a century before you were born—a very long time ago. Yet even today, the name Adolf Hitler and images of concentration camps, Japanese prisoner of war camps, and atom bombs fill many hearts with dread.

Hitler was a cruel and dangerous man who drove his followers to commit incredible atrocities. The Nazis murdered millions of civilians: 6 million Jews as well as other groups Hitler deemed inferior to Germans, such as Russians and Poles. But Second World War horrors also took place in Asia. Torture, insufficient food, and poor sanitary conditions at many Japanese prisoner of war (POW) camps killed large numbers of Allies. And the Second World War presented humanity with a new and terrifying horror: the atomic bomb. Some argue that dropping the A-bomb on Japan shortened the war. Certainly it introduced a scale of destruction never before seen. These bombs were the forerunners of the weapons of mass destruction that we so fear today.

On September 1, 1939, the Germans stunned the world by invading Poland. The German army crushed the Poles in just a few days. Most countries did not want to fight a war. Memories of the First World War, in which 9 million military lives were lost and so much of Europe was destroyed, were strong. But there was another reason most of the world was unprepared: the Great Depression. During the 1930s, many governments were preoccupied with trying to find food and work for their citizens who were jobless and hungry.

In Germany, meanwhile, Hitler spent most of the 1930s building the armed forces and ordering factories to produce war materials. He also took the first steps in the creation of his empire. He reoccupied the Rhineland in 1936 (which Germany had been forbidden to occupy

"Heute gehört uns Deutschland
Today, Germany is Ours;
Morgen die ganze Welt!"
Tomorrow, the Whole World

OH, YEAH?

Books cannot be killed by fire.

People die, but books never die. No man and no force can put thought in a concentration camp forever. No man and no force can take from the world the books that embody man's eternal fight against tyranny. In this war, we know, books are weapons. Franklin D. Roosevelt

BOOKS ARE WEAPONS IN THE WAR OF IDEAS

This poster was produced by the U.S. Office of War Information in 1942.

after the First World War), annexed Austria in 1938, and then began to seize Czechoslovakia later the same year. Hitler claimed that all he wanted to do was bring the German-speaking people under one government—his. But when the Nazis invaded Poland in September 1939, it was finally clear that he had to be stopped or all of Europe would fall. Two days later, Great Britain, France, Australia, New Zealand, and India declared war on Germany. Canada followed suit a week later.

The next spring (1940), Germany invaded one country after another. Denmark, Norway, Belgium, the Netherlands, and France all fell before the German advance. Italy, which had signed a non-aggression pact with Germany in 1939, now declared war on the Allies. The Nazis occupied or had control over most of western Europe, and the British feared their country would be next. The Germans did indeed bomb Britain's airfields and cities very heavily in August and September 1940 (the Battle of

Britain). They also attempted to cut off Great Britain's supplies arriving by sea. But the British, led by Prime Minister Winston Churchill, refused to surrender.

In the spring of 1941, Hitler turned his focus to the eastern front: the Union of Soviet Socialist Republics (also known as Russia). First, Germany, Italy, Hungary, and Bulgaria occupied Yugoslavia and Greece to ensure the Allies would not attack Hitler's armies as they pushed eastward. Then, in June, German armies attacked the Russians. After a few months, Hitler realized that the Russians were much tougher than he had thought. He had believed the conflict would be over by Christmas 1941, but the Russians continued to fight. With the onset of frigid winter conditions, many German troops died from hunger and cold.

To make matters worse for Hitler, Japan attacked Pearl Harbor, Hawaii, on December 7, 1941. The Japanese emperor, Hirohito, wanted to destroy the U.S. fleet to keep the Americans

People in occupied Europe listened to British radio broadcasts in secret.

from hindering the expansion of his empire. The United States responded by declaring war on Japan. Germany was then forced to declare war on the U.S. because Germany had signed a pact with Japan in 1940 that promised that if one country was attacked, the other would help defend it. Now all the world's major powers were at war. What's more, Americans were on their way to Europe to fight the Nazis.

The Second World War was waged on land, on sea, and in the air. The Axis and Allies fought around the world. The war lasted six years and cost more in financial terms than any war before it. But even worse was the huge loss of life: at least 30 million people died. (That's more than live in Canada or California today.) In Europe, the war finally ended on May 8, 1945—VE (Victory in Europe) day. Four months later, the war ended in Asia on September 2, 1945—VJ (Victory over Japan) day.

When the war started, many feared that Germany was undefeatable. But as the Allies waged war, it became apparent that many factors would shape the outcome. This book looks at the ways in which creative thinking, daring schemes, and clever deception helped change the course of history. The stories of the people involved and their commitment to influence the destiny of their world are lasting tributes to courage and ingenuity. The U.S. 23rd Headquarters Special Troops, for example, invented fake weapons—such as dummy Sherman tanks made of inflatable rubber—that helped the Allies win battles in France. The invasion of Italy was successful in large part because of a British ploy whereby a dead soldier convinced Hitler that the Allies were about to land in Greece rather than Sicily. The Allies lured the Germans into traps, tricked enemy commanders into believing lies, and hid their intentions from their opponents—trickery that helped the Allies defeat a stronger foe. But the Allies had to be on their guard as the Germans used tricks too!

Other stories profile the freedom fighters who risked everything to resist the enemy. Many of them were ordinary people, civilians like Tony Brooks and his cohorts, who "repaired" the bearings on railway flatcars with a special paste that made the wheels seize up after a few miles of travel. The Germans were furious! They had planned to use the flatcars to carry tanks and armored vehicles to reinforce their troops just after D-Day. Resistance groups proved it was possible for courageous heroes to obstruct the Germans in spite of the enemy's large numbers and powerful weapons.

Would the Allies win or lose? Imagination and courage helped shift the balance.

DECEPTION

The odds favored Germany in 1939. The German armed forces were well trained and equipped; it would take years for the Allies to catch up. Before that happened, the Nazis would surely defeat them … unless the Allies could use their wits to fool the enemy into thinking they were stronger than they really were, or to trick the enemy into making choices that would help the Allied cause. Deception was one way to even the odds.

Deceiving the enemy often required unusual talent. A British company that specialized in making movie sets helped build decoy towns and airfields to confuse German aircraft dropping bombs over Great Britain during 1940–41. The British wanted the bombers to mistake the phony sites for real ones. In another ruse, British radio broadcasters deliberately misled the enemy. Pretending to be German, they told listeners that they would soon be forced out of their homes, and that German officers were deserting, hoping to undermine their audience's faith in their Nazi government. The Allies also used trickery during the invasion of Sicily. Bogus radio traffic, false radar signals, and phony landing noises diverted the enemy's attention away from the true assault happening miles away.

A dummy anti-aircraft gun and gunner in the Western Desert. The figure on the right is not a dummy but Lieutenant W.J. Wilkie.

The Germans deceived the Allies, too. In the spring of 1941, German soldiers studied English while their officers gossiped loudly in bars about a planned invasion, leading spies to guess that Germany would soon attack England. The Russians were surprised when the Germans actually invaded the Soviet Union that June!

One of the most amazing Allied deceptions was a phantom army. It was a fake American force supposedly preparing to attack France in the Pas de Calais, the shortest distance across the English Channel from Great Britain. This army consisted of phony units with real insignias. Its bogus equipment looked authentic from the air. What's more, a general who was respected and feared by the Germans was said to be the phantom army's leader. The Allies hoped the Germans would wait for the non-existent army to attack the Pas de Calais instead of sending reinforcements to Normandy on D-Day, June 6, 1944. Would the ruse give American, British, and Canadian troops time to gain a foothold on French soil … or would the Germans catch on to the trick in time to halt the invasion?

Deception tactics were to play a key role in the war's outcome.

ALLIED INVASION OF SICILY

More than two months after Major Martin's body was found drifting off the coast of Spain, eight American and British divisions landed on Sicily. It was July 10, 1943. Although the seas were rough, the assault went well, the second-largest amphibious landing of the Second World War (after Operation Overlord, the invasion of Normandy).

The American Seventh Army under General George Patton and the British Eighth Army under General Sir Bernard Montgomery fought for 38 days, hoping to trap Axis troops—mostly Italian—on the island. But when they reached the port of Messina, only three miles (5 km) from the Italian mainland, they discovered that many had escaped across the Messina Strait. The invasion was still a success, however. The central Mediterranean was now safe for shipping Allied supplies, and the Axis retreat hastened the resignation of the Italian dictator, Mussolini. By August 19, newly appointed Italian prime minister Marshal Badoglio had begun discussing surrender terms with the Allies.

DEAD RINGER

Tricking the enemy into believing a lie can be nerve-racking—not to mention dangerous. One tiny slip-up and ... zap! the illusion is shattered. Every invented fact must be believable and every detail must fit perfectly; a blunder could cost your side lives.

One of the most ingenious British deceptions was Operation Mincemeat, carried out in 1943. The Allies (including British and American troops) had just defeated the Axis (mainly German and Italian troops) in North Africa. The next battleground seemed obvious to many: the island of Sicily on Italy's southwestern coast. Sicily was the closest Axis-held land across the Mediterranean Sea from North Africa. (See Allied Invasion of Sicily, left.) The trick was to convince the Axis that the Allies were going to attack Greece and Sardinia instead.

Constructing this ruse was a lot like writing a movie script. But the brilliant twist in the plot was that a corpse would play the leading role. The British would control the first few scenes, then could only hope that the players on the Axis side would perform their parts as predicted, producing a successful ending for the Allies.

First, the British had to find the main character. Coming up with any old dead body was easy enough (after all, this was wartime), but finding the right corpse was a challenge. The perfect leading man needed to be slightly out of shape and in his thirties—able to pass for a staff officer in the Royal Marines (a credible courier of secret information). He also needed to appear to have drowned after a plane crash in the ocean. Furthermore, he needed a family willing to release his body to the military, no questions asked; everything had to be kept top-secret.

Just when the project seemed hopeless, a body turned up in London, a pneumonia victim whose fluid-filled lungs might convince the German high command that he had drowned at sea and floated in a life jacket for several days. The corpse was immediately preserved in dry ice, not quite ready yet to go to war. First, the body needed to join the Royal Marines. It joined as Captain (acting Major) William Martin. One of the most common surnames in the service was chosen so that the dead man might easily be mistaken for any of the real Martins, adding to his authenticity. To develop Martin's life and personality, he was given identity papers, service ribbons, theater ticket stubs, money, receipts, personal letters—even love letters from a

Generals Montgomery (left) and Patton (right) shake hands

ALLIES BUT RIVALS

During the Sicilian campaign, a rivalry developed between General George Patton and General Sir Bernard Montgomery. Their armies had "raced" to Messina, the Americans reaching the port a few hours before the British. When the Eighth Army arrived, they were greeted by teasing Seventh Army troops who called them "tourists." A year later, the competition between the two generals intensified in France during the Allied invasion of northwest Europe. They frequently urged different approaches and vied for supplies.

ARMY, NAVY, OR MARINES?

Deciding which service Martin should "join" took careful thought. A simple slip-up could bungle the whole ruse. For instance, enlisting him in the army might set off alarm bells, because death reports of army officers were automatically distributed to several departments, increasing the risk that someone might become suspicious. However, if Martin joined the navy, the Director of Naval Intelligence could order that all questions about his death be sent directly to the intelligence officers who already knew about the trick.

Ah, but navy uniforms were made to measure, which meant a tailor would have to measure the dead body—a definite breach of security! Luckily, the Royal Marines, a service within the navy, wore battledress, which was not tailored. Problem solved? Not completely. Royal Marines carried photo ID cards. The British had to find a live double for the picture.

phantom girlfriend. Carefully crafted details made it appear that Martin hadn't left London until April 24.

In fact, Major Martin, traveling in a special container packed with dry ice, left England on April 19 aboard a submarine. Chained to his wrist was the reason for the ruse: a locked briefcase with bogus official documents and two fake personal letters. The first was from one senior officer to another, stating that Martin, an expert on landing craft, was flying from England to Allied headquarters in North Africa. The second letter subtly suggested that two Allied attacks would be launched in the Mediterranean, one in Greece, the other in Sardinia.

The British reasoned that a chained briefcase would be so important-looking that the enemy would surely search it. But they were lucky this trick didn't give them away! British officers never chained briefcases to their wrists. Luckily, the Germans didn't know that.

Just before dawn 11 days after leaving England, the submarine surfaced about a mile off the coast of Huelva, Spain. Crewmen, who had no clue what they were carrying, brought Martin's container topside. The captain sent the crewmen back below, then quickly briefed his officers on the hoax. They prepared Martin for launch, inflating his life jacket and making sure the briefcase was securely attached to its chain, then slipped him over the side. A few hours later, a fishing boat picked up the dead marine and took him into port. (The script was being followed to a T!)

When notified of the washed-up body, the British vice-consul in Spain demanded that the Spanish government turn over the briefcase, unopened and intact. But the Spaniards refused, claiming they were holding it for "judicial purposes." In reality, they were informing the Abwehr. The British knew this was what the Spanish would do. Although Spain was nominally neutral, the Spanish government owed Germany limited allegiance because Hitler had helped Spain's dictator gain power during the Spanish Civil War (1936–39).

By listening in on German radio traffic, the British learned that the Abwehr next checked the body for authenticity, notified the German high command in Berlin, photographed the documents, and then gave everything back to the Spanish officials to return to the Allies. (Great! The enemy was acting as planned!)

Tanks are loaded onto transport ships in preparation for the invasion of Sicily

Meanwhile, the corpse's name appeared on the next British casualty list, and it later showed up in British newspapers alongside the names of two officers who had really perished in a plane at sea. In Huelva, Martin was buried with full military honors. His phantom fiancée sent a funeral wreath and a heartbroken card of remembrance, and photographs were sent to his family of the Spanish naval salute at his graveside. (The Abwehr's spies, of course, took note of all this.)

After stalling, the Spanish government returned Martin's briefcase, apparently unopened. However, by this time the British had already intercepted German military communications which confirmed that the Abwehr believed the documents to be the real thing. The German high command bought it too. And as the Allies had hoped, Hitler played his part perfectly. As well as moving some troops, he assigned one of his top generals to command the defense of Greece. Pleased with the operation so far, the British chiefs of staff sent a message to Prime Minister Winston Churchill that read, "Mincemeat Swallowed Whole."

When the Allies stormed Sicily on July 10, they caught the Germans and Italians almost completely by surprise. By August 17, the British and Americans had taken the island. Operation Mincemeat was truly a success.

MARTIN'S PERSONAL EFFECTS

British intelligence must have had fun dreaming up believable "evidence" for Martin's briefcase and pockets. Here are some of the items the Abwehr found:

✔ an out-of-date pass to enter Combined Operations HQ

✔ an invitation to a nightclub, provided by a staff member who had an actual invitation

✔ a letter concerning an overdraft, provided by the joint general manager of Lloyds Bank, sent to Martin at the Naval and Military Club, 94 Piccadilly, but addressed to Army and Navy Club, Pall Mall, and finished with a handwritten note, "Not known at this address. Try Naval and Military Club, 94 Piccadilly"

✔ a bill from Naval and Military Club, 94 Piccadilly

✔ a receipt for an engagement ring from S.J. Phillips Jewellers, chosen because the company traded internationally, which meant the Germans could get an authentic receipt to compare it with

✔ a photo of his fiancée, Pam, provided by a woman in the office

✔ love letters from Pam, written by another woman in the office and aged by repeatedly folding, refolding, and rubbing—but not crumpling. Martin would never crumple a cherished letter; that would look like an obvious attempt to age the paper.

✔ correspondence with his father and solicitors on appropriate letterhead

✔ two ticket stubs from the Prince of Wales theater for April 22. Since the body actually left England on the 19th, the tickets helped "prove" that Martin had left London at a later date. British intelligence obtained advance tickets through normal channels.

AMPHIBIOUS LANDING: *an operation in which ship-borne troops land on an enemy-held coastal area*

GROUND COVER

It sounds crazy…but it was cunning. A branch of the British Air Ministry actually wanted the Germans to drop bombs on their airfields. In fact, the more hits the better. Of course, it was a trick. The British were luring the Luftwaffe (German air force) into attacking special decoys rather than real airfields, factories, and towns.

The ruse began in autumn 1939, just days after Great Britain had declared war on Germany. The Germans had overpowered Poland in less than a month. The United Kingdom might soon suffer the same fate, and the British military were certain that Germany's first attacks would come from the air, to knock out the Royal Air Force (RAF). Protecting Britain's air bases was crucial.

But how? It would be impossible to completely hide an airfield, with its many buildings, hangars, and aircraft. Camouflage would help, but the Air Ministry had a trickier idea: create bogus airfields. The Luftwaffe might think the imitations were among the many satellite airfields—a grass runway, a few huts, and a couple of aircraft—that were springing up as the British prepared for war.

To spearhead this project, the Air Ministry needed an effective, imaginative leader. Fortunately, they had one: Colonel John F. Turner, then head of the ministry's Department of Works. Turner called his new group Colonel Turner's Department (CTD), quite an unimaginative name. In fact, it was a sly title because it didn't give anything away—and helped keep the department's doings a mystery.

Soon, many farmers' fields became "K sites," a label that disguised their true purpose. CTD created fake truck and airplane tracks by mowing fields, killing vegetation with bleach, or creating paths with sand or straw. But what the phony airfields really needed were authentic-looking airplanes. Unfortunately, the aircraft industry's cost estimates for building mock-ups were much too high. Besides, factories needed to concentrate on building real planes.

Undaunted, CTD came up with a brilliant solution: ask the film industry to help. After all,

1940s FLIGHT NAVIGATION

Unless Second World War pilots could positively identify a landmark, they were often unsure of their exact location. Navigation was a haphazard science during the Second World War. A pilot, or his navigator if he had one, calculated the plane's location by noting its speed and the direction the compass needle was pointing, with adjustments for the speed and direction of the wind. For example, a plane flying at 200 miles per hour (320 k.p.h.) might actually be crossing only 180 miles (290 km) over the ground. Also, if the plane was pointing west but the wind was blowing north, the plane could be traveling northwest. Navigators used a sextant to estimate their longitude and latitude, particularly useful on clear nights when the North Star was visible. Even so, navigation aids were so elementary that pilots sometimes landed in the wrong country!

AVIATION SEXTANT: an instrument used to estimate a plane's longitude and latitude by measuring the angles of the sun, moon, and stars to the earth

Camouflage nets were mesh with short strips of cloth dyed to match the color of the landscape, tied in random patterns, and sometimes covered with leaves or straw. They were draped over equipment and supplies— tanks, jeeps, guns, tents, and bunkers—to conceal them from enemy aircraft.

IN LIKE KIND

The Germans too used decoy and camouflage techniques to fool the enemy. One effective trick was to conceal rivers and bridges by covering them with camouflage nets. Then, using straw mats, the Germans built fake bridges over other rivers, a few miles from the real ones. They also covered railway stations with straw mats to make the buildings look like roads from the air. Very clever! And yet, surprisingly, German decoy airfields were not well done. The Allies easily discovered them because reconnaissance photos revealed that the "aircraft" on the fake runways never moved.

PATHFINDER RAIDS

On night missions over Germany, elite pathfinder squadrons flew ahead of the main RAF bomber stream, dropping target indicators (flares and incendiaries) that helped the pilots behind them locate the objective. To counteract this, the Germans designed rockets that burned like indicators. They fired them between the time of the pathfinder raid and the arrival of the main force, drawing the bombers away from the real target.

they were experts at whipping up cheap but realistic scenery and props. Sound City Films tackled the project with gusto, producing "genuine" aircraft for 36 K sites by the summer of 1940. The first mock-ups were flat, made of wood, and set on trestles to create realistic shadows that were convincing from the air. Later models were constructed of inflatable tubing and canvas, which could be rolled up into a bag when moved.

As it turned out, K sites were a disappointment. They required too many workers—often as many as 24—to move the "aircraft" from spot to spot, to make new tracks, and to run around during an air raid like workers at a real airfield. Also, authentic satellite fields were becoming larger and more permanent, which made them harder to copy. The final blow came in October 1941, when a captured Luftwaffe map revealed that the Germans knew most of the K sites were frauds.

Nighttime targets were easier to imitate. The main props were lights—simple and cheap. It was a great idea … except that the first lights, paraffin flares tried in late 1939, created a new danger. They couldn't be extinguished quickly enough to discourage friendly aircraft from landing, and the RAF didn't want their own planes crashing into dummy airfields!

By June 1940, effective night decoys (Q sites) were up and running. Lines of electric lights mimicked runways, and could be dimmed just like real airfields trying to hide from the enemy. In addition, headlights suspended on movable wires appeared from the air to be taxiing and landing aircraft. Special signals, such as the presence or absence of certain lights, warned RAF aircraft to land elsewhere. Two men controlled the entire "air station" from a bunker. When informed by radar station operators that enemy bombers were approaching, the controllers carefully calculated the moment the enemy should have spotted them, then switched off the lights, "carelessly" leaving one or two on. The ploy often worked. Fully half of the Luftwaffe night attacks on airfields fell on Q sites.

After a few months, the Luftwaffe began bombing

industrial and civil targets, so CTD created QL sites, each one tailored specifically for the building or buildings it was protecting. For example, if the site was imitating a factory, it might fake the flare behind opened furnace doors. If it was pretending to be a town, light might escape the way it did through cracks in curtains during a blackout.

But a further deception was needed. When the Luftwaffe hit a true target, fires lit up the sky, making it easy for the next wave of pilots to locate the target. The British extinguished fires at real sites as quickly as possible, then CTD set bonfires in sparsely inhabited areas to lure the bombers that followed. CTD set up special sites— QF for military and SF (or Starfish) for civilian—all over Britain. Bonfires imitated the kinds of blazes the Luftwaffe would expect to see, such as the dazzling white flames of a boiler fire or the deep red glow of a coal fire.

Starfish sites—eventually 209 in all—were constructed close to all British cities and major towns. Every British citizen who could contributed burnable materials. Tons of wood and other combustibles were soaked in flammables such as oil, paraffin, and creosote to create dramatic fires that looked as random and varied as a burning city. But everyone was safe, even the men who set the blazes, because the fires were ignited from bunkers about 600 yards (540 m) away.

Colonel Turner's Department's trickery saved many lives and military installations. Furthermore, CTD's efforts boosted British morale.

BATTLE OF BRITAIN

After the Germans occupied France in June 1940, Hitler began to plan Operation Sea Lion, the invasion of Britain. The Luftwaffe would have to defeat both the Royal Air Force and the Royal Navy before an amphibious invasion was possible (the German navy was too weak), and Hitler decided to attack the Royal Air Force first. Beginning on August 13, 1940, which the Germans called Eagle Day, Germany assaulted targets they knew RAF pilots would rush to defend, such as coastal convoys, radar stations, aircraft factories, and RAF airfields. The Luftwaffe nearly destroyed the RAF—but they didn't know it. The Germans were deceived into believing the RAF to be much stronger than it actually was.

To the relief of the British, the Germans switched their strategy in the middle of September. The Luftwaffe began to raid London and other urban centers at night. These raids became known as the Blitz.

Two factors helped save Great Britain. For one, radar warned the British of approaching raids, allowing them to get their own planes into the air in time to defeat the attackers. A second advantage was that the RAF fought over home territory, so when British pilots were shot down, they could fight again. Downed German pilots became prisoners of war.

Great Britain had narrowly escaped invasion and defeat. In Prime Minister Winston Churchill's words of praise for the RAF pilots, "Never in the field of human conflict was so much owed by so many to so few."

DID THE DECOYS WORK?

The Luftwaffe attacked day decoys (K sites and dummy factories) 47 times, Q sites 521 times, and Starfish sites 119 times. In 1942, decoy sites drew 9.95 percent of the 2,761 tons of bombs dropped on Great Britain. Over the entire war, decoys drew an estimated 5 percent of the 68,500 tons of bombs directed at Great Britain. They likely saved over 2,500 lives.

WORKING MAGIC

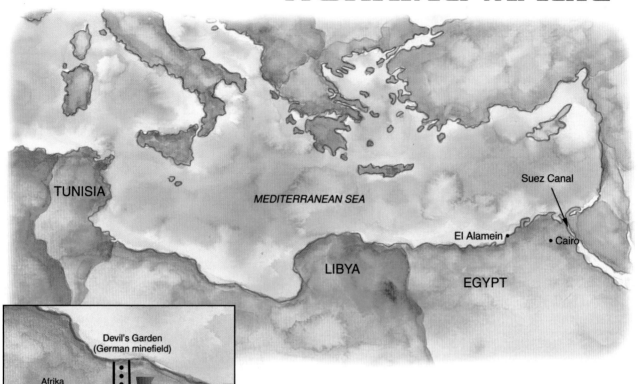

TUNISIA

MEDITERRANEAN SEA

Suez Canal

El Alamein •

• Cairo

LIBYA

EGYPT

Devil's Garden
(German minefield)

Afrika
Korps
(German)

Eighth
Army
(British)

QATTARA DEPRESSION

WAR IN THE WESTERN DESERT

In June 1940, Italy declared war on Great Britain. Three months later, Italian troops crossed the border of Libya (an Italian colony) into Egypt (a British protectorate). The British fought back, nearly ejecting the Italians from North Africa in early 1941. Almost immediately, Hitler sent the Afrika Korps, commanded by General Erwin Rommel, to assist the Italians. Hitler had also secretly instructed Rommel to seize Cairo and the Suez Canal, then to take the entire Middle East, including the region's valuable oil fields.

Rommel, nicknamed the Desert Fox, was a gifted strategist. Within two weeks, he drove the British back over the Egyptian border. In November 1941, Prime Minister Churchill appointed General

Continued on page 20

iddle Eastern oil: that was the prize the Nazis were after in North Africa in 1942—fuel for Axis warships, tanks, and aircraft. To get it, Hitler needed to capture the Suez Canal, the waterway that cut through Egypt from the Mediterranean to the Red Sea. It was the shortest sea route between thirsty European war machines and flowing Middle Eastern oil fields.

For two years, the Axis and Allied armies had pushed each other back and forth across the coastal region of Libya and Egypt known as the Western Desert. When one side had food, fuel, and ammunition, it pushed forward, only to retreat when it was far from its base and supplies ran low. (See War in the Western Desert, left.) Now it was early autumn 1942. Hitler's Afrika Korps was less than 250 miles (400 km) west of the Suez Canal—only two days away.

The British Eighth Army had retreated to El Alamein, a way station for the railway running along the Mediterranean coast. To the south lay the Qattara Depression, a lifeless, impassable area of salt flats. With the sea on one end and the depression on the other, the front was only 40 miles (65 km) wide.

It was the Afrika Korps's turn to run low on supplies. But instead of retreating entirely, German field marshal

The German general Erwin Rommel, a brilliant tactician, was known as the Desert Fox.

Claude Auchinleck leader of the newly enlarged Eighth Army, now trained to fight Rommel's fast-moving and aggressive style of tank warfare. In a heated, month-long battle, both sides suffered heavy losses. The Afrika Korps had superior anti-tank guns (the dual-purpose 88 mm) and better tanks. But by early December, the British began pushing the Axis back to where Rommel had been the previous February.

Then new supplies reached Rommel. In May, he renewed his offensive, pushing the Eighth Army back over the Egyptian border. The British retreated to El Alamein on the Mediterranean coast, only a morning's journey from Cairo by car. The first battle of El Alamein began on July 1, 1942. Neither side prevailed, so both settled back to regroup for the next battle.

In early August, General Sir Bernard Montgomery took command of the Eighth Army. Churchill believed Auchinleck was too cautious a general to defeat Rommel's spectacular, daring tactics. As it turned out, Montgomery too was careful, but he was also persistent. Montgomery waited for better equipment, raised his troops' spirits, and trained his men well. Meanwhile, the Afrika Korps failed to receive new supplies. Less than two weeks after the Eighth Army took the Afrika Korps by surprise at the second battle at El Alamein on October 23, the Afrika Korps began its long retreat to Tunisia. (See Working Magic, page 18.)

Erwin Rommel masterminded a new strategy. He reasoned that the Allies' next assault would be at the northern end of the front, close to the Mediterranean coast and the region's only highway. Rommel ordered his men to lay an enormous minefield in the north, called the Devil's Garden. It ran from the Mediterranean Sea to the Qattara Depression, and on average was five miles (8 km) wide. It contained more than half a million land mines. If the Allies tried to clear a corridor or two through the minefield, they would have to do it on foot, ahead of their tanks. Meanwhile, the Afrika Korps lying in wait on the nearby ridge would wipe them out.

Rommel underestimated the British Eighth Army's new leader, General Sir Bernard Montgomery. Monty, as he was known, was a careful planner who kept the morale of his troops high. He was now waiting for fresh anti-tank artillery and the latest model Sherman tanks.

The British had another advantage: Monty knew of Rommel's plans. The British had been secretly decoding German messages. Rommel had guessed correctly that the British would attack in the north, but Montgomery hoped to trick him into believing otherwise. Somehow he must convince Rommel that the Eighth Army would attack in the south. If the Germans moved in that direction, it would give the British time to clear two tank corridors through the Devil's Garden.

But how to make the real buildup of troops in the north look harmless, and phony divisions in the south look menacing? The British turned to Jasper Maskelyne, an English stage magician and a member of A Force, a brigade that specialized in deception. He and his Magic Gang—a ragtag mixture of film technicians, writers, and painters—were masters of light, shadow, and illusion.

In Maskelyne's makeshift desert workshop, the Magic Gang turned out incredible illusions using cheap, lightweight construction materials. For the phony troop buildup in the south, the gang covered real jeeps and trucks with dummy tanks made of plywood and painted canvas. The dummies were only partially hidden with camouflage netting so the enemy would see them. For added realism, truck wheels were altered to simulate tank tracks.

The Magic Gang also constructed a phony pipeline to supply the mock army in the south. (An invading force would need water, and a pipeline would be like a giant arrow pointing at the troops, sure to be seen by German reconnaissance planes flying overhead.) They built the pipeline with oil cans, making sure its progress could be spotted by German planes. They also placed a supply dump at the end of the pipeline to create the impression that troops in the south had plenty of food and ammunition. In fact, the "dump" was really camouflage nets and flat steel wool that looked like shadows in the smooth desert. Amazingly, it appeared three-dimensional from the air.

A dummy truck, made from sacking and bamboo

The Magic Gang worked slowly to make the Germans believe they weren't in a rush. The British wanted the Germans to think the attack was scheduled for November.

The Germans had watched closely. They were so convinced by the charade that Rommel flew to Austria in October for a brief sick leave, which he probably would not have done if he thought an attack was coming, even though he required medical treatment.

Maskelyne and his men also worked their magic in the north, where they needed to make it look like a small number of Allied troops were there to keep the enemy from breaking through and attacking from behind. But they wanted the Germans to believe the Allies were focusing on the much greater buildup in the south, so the challenge in the north was to conceal real tanks, ammunition, and other supplies.

At night, little by little, they moved tanks north, slipping them under plywood shields already in position that made them look like supply trucks from the air. They then swept away the tank tracks. By next morning, the area looked the same to German air reconnaissance as it had the day before. To conceal boxes of supplies, the military wizards piled them in truck shapes, then covered them with camouflage netting. Tents, supposedly housing for the soldiers who drove the fake trucks, really hid more

TURNING POINT

British prime minister Winston Churchill believed that the October 23–November 3, 1942, Battle of El Alamein (the second battle at El Alamein in four months) marked a turning point of the Second World War. By his orders, church bells rang all over Great Britain on November 15—the first time the bells had rung since the beginning of the war. Later, Churchill wrote in his book *The Hinge of Fate*: "Before Alamein we never had a victory. After Alamein we never had a defeat."

RECONNAISSANCE: *a look at something to gain information*

Sherman M4

SHERMAN M4

The Sherman M4 was an American tank built by Chrysler Motors. Eleven plants produced a total of nearly 50,000 tanks between 1942 and 1945. The British Eighth Army used them first at El Alamein. Later, they became the mainstay of Allied operations in Europe.

The most common version of the Sherman M4 weighed a crushing 66,500 pounds (30,000 kg). Its maximum speed was 26 miles (42 km) per hour; its range, 100 miles (160 km). It carried a crew of five.

The original featured a 75-mm gun that fired both armor-piercing and high-explosive shells. Some of these were replaced in late spring 1944 with a 76-mm high-velocity gun, still inferior to its German counterpart, the 88-mm anti-tank gun. The Sherman's armor was also second-rate, not as thick as the metal covering German tanks. However, the Sherman M4 was maneuverable, and it was more mechanically reliable and easier to service than German tanks.

MINE: *an explosive device buried underground*

boxes of supplies. To make the phony vehicles look real, British troops drove trucks around to create tire tracks.

Maskelyne and his Magic Gang deserved a round of applause; their performance turned out to be a winning one. On the night of October 23, 1942, the Allies took the Axis by surprise. Allied troops attacked in the south to divert the enemy's attention. Then, up near the Mediterranean coast, about 1,000 Allied field guns roared all at once. The sky was ablaze. Under the almost full moon, troops walked forward holding their rifles fixed with bayonets ready for battle. Others probed the ground with their bayonets or swept the area with mine detectors. Carefully, they removed tripwires and booby traps. The air began to thicken with dust as the attackers and defenders exchanged fire and mines exploded. Behind, waiting Allied tanks and trucks inched forward.

By October 24, Axis headquarters was in total disarray. The bombardment had cut the communication lines between the Axis armored units and their high command. On the evening of October 24, Hitler phoned Rommel, who was still recuperating in Europe; he told the general to return to North Africa. The first battle reports that Rommel received were confusing: the British seemed to be attacking all along the 40-mile (65 km) front! However, Rommel was not fooled for long. He quickly realized that the most significant Allied gains had been made in the north. One armored division had already made it through the minefield.

By the time Rommel flew into North Africa on the evening of October 25, Montgomery had the upper hand. Now that Allied tanks and anti-tank guns were on the Axis side of the Devil's Garden, they were in a strong position to damage the Afrika Korps's remaining tanks and force them to retreat.

Ten days later, the Afrika Korps did withdraw westward towards Libya and eventually into Tunisia. The back-and-forth battles across the Western Desert were finally over. The Germans surrendered in North Africa in May 1943.

FALSE FRONT

W hat a nightmare! In August 1939, Adolf Hitler and Joseph Stalin signed a pact. They promised that neither Germany nor Russia would invade the other. But in secret parts of the treaty, both leaders agreed to build their nations into empires, dividing Europe between them. Unbelievable! Two tyrants with opposing political beliefs were working together to control the continent.

But were they really friends? Behind the pact lay hidden agendas. Hitler's true objective was to overrun Poland without Soviet opposition and then to storm the Soviet Union later. Meanwhile, he'd let the Soviets believe they were cohorts. As it turned out, Stalin was wily too. He intended to grab territory in eastern Europe and make it part of the Soviet Union. Although Stalin understood the Nazi's intention to eventually break the pact, he meant to forestall the assault for as long as possible.

A week after the pact was signed, the Nazis trounced Poland. Within a month, Hitler rewarded Stalin for not opposing the attack, allowing Soviet armies to seize eastern Poland. By June 1940, Hitler controlled most of western Europe and the Soviets had snatched parts of eastern and northern Europe. (See Soviet Union, page 26.)

The big question now: what country would Hitler seize next? According to Stalin's calculations, Great Britain. He believed Hitler would wait until summer 1942 to expand eastward into Russia. Wrong! Actually, Hitler planned to

> **FRONT:** *a line of battle on which advance or defense is based*

EASTERN FRONT

Hitler hated Communism and wanted to snuff it out. What's more, he coveted Russia's resources: timber forests, grain fields, and raw materials such as oil and iron. After a swift June 1941 invasion, the Nazis thought the German armies would easily defeat the Soviets before Christmas. Three million German soldiers—along with half a million Axis troops from Italy, Finland, Hungary, Romania, Slovakia, and Croatia—attacked Russia. The battle line, known as the eastern front, stretched 1,800 miles (2,700 km) from the Baltic Sea in the north to the Black Sea in the south.

The Russians turned out to be a formidable foe. By December, German troops were exhausted, cold, and hungry. They had reached the outskirts of Moscow, 1,000 miles (1,600 km) from Berlin. Their supplies were low and, even worse, army planners had failed to equip them for winter warfare. The Soviets now launched a major counterattack,

Continued on page 25

launch Operation Barbarossa—code name for the invasion of the Soviet Union—in mid-May 1941 to give his military plenty of time to take control of the country before the harsh Russian winter set in.

The Germans wanted to keep the operation a secret, but it was impossible to conceal troops building up on the Soviet border. So the Nazis created an elaborate ruse to convince the Russians that the bulk of German forces were in the West, and that any troops in the East were there to trick Great Britain into thinking it wouldn't be attacked. If the Soviets didn't believe that story, the Nazis intended to claim the German deployments were defensive.

The Nazis knew that to convince the Soviets they were still comrades, they had to do more than simply tell them lies. They decided to shore up the phony truth with rumors and misleading clues. Russian and British spies could be anywhere: embassies, train stations, the marketplace, even the armed forces. Convincing these agents was crucial.

High-ranking officers kept their own troops in the dark to make sure enemy agents would not learn the real facts from them. Some German soldiers really did believe that Operation Barbarossa was a backup plan in case the Russians attacked Germany. Others believed they had been transferred to the East to confuse the British into thinking the Germans were about to invade the Soviet Union. To add credibility, soldiers on the eastern front studied English vocabulary and geography. If German soldiers believed they would soon be shipped westward, then loose-lipped chatter with local civilians or spies might include stories about their English lessons.

Fake information traveled the airwaves, too. Imaginary forces sent radio messages that it was hoped British or Russian spies would intercept. To make sure German troops didn't mistake these messages for the real thing, they contained a special prefix. The Nazis knew that spies gathered intelligence from German armed forces radio, so they aired phony song requests and personal messages on Sundays for soldiers supposedly stationed in the West, to create the illusion that troops had already moved westward.

To further convince the Soviets and the Allies, Nazis skillfully spread gossip. In Berlin, foreign agents were known to snoop around wholesale markets and newspaper distribution centers, so these were perfect places for the Nazis to plant "evidence." Stories of soon to be discontinued westerly train routes hinted that civilian travel in that direction would be cut

driving the Germans away from Moscow.

Throughout the next spring and summer, the Germans fought back. By September 1942, Nazi domination had reached its peak. It stretched from France in the west to the Volga River in the east, and from the Arctic Circle in the north to North Africa in the south.

Two months later, the Soviet army launched a massive counteroffensive. Fought over the winter of 1942–43, the five-month battle for Stalingrad was a major turning point of the war. The Germans destroyed the city, but the Soviets refused to give in. Eventually, the Soviets began pushing the Germans westward. As the Soviet army advanced, it liberated many German-occupied countries, including Poland. When it reached the Romanian border, Romania joined the Soviets to fight the Nazis.

Russian troops finally crossed the German border in August 1944. But the costs had been huge: an estimated 20 million Soviet citizens died between 1941 and 1944, half of them civilians.

The following April, the Soviets encircled Berlin, Hitler's headquarters. Hitler committed suicide on April 30, 1945, and two days later Berlin surrendered to Soviet forces.

The caption on this Soviet poster reads: "Long live the powerful air forces of the Socialist countries."

SOVIET UNION

The Soviet Union—officially the Union of Soviet Socialist Republics—was also known as the USSR and Russia. At the beginning of the Second World War, the Soviet Union consisted of 11 republics, of which Russia was by far the biggest. In fact, it was, and still is, the largest country in the world, covering half of Europe and nearly half of Asia. By the end of the war, the USSR contained 15 republics.

For hundreds of years, a czar—an emperor—ruled Russia. He had enormous power over the lives of Russians, who were mainly poor, uneducated peasants living on tiny farms. By the turn of the twentieth century, most of Europe was becoming industrialized, but Russia was still an undeveloped nation. A few educated Russians had studied Karl Marx's theories and believed that natural and industrial resources should be owned by everyone. This would ultimately bring about a classless society with no rich and no poor.

The Marxists appealed to peasants, who needed more land, and to factory workers, who wanted more pay and shorter workdays. In 1917, during the First World War, war-weary Russians drove the czar from power. A few months later, the Bolsheviks (later called Communists), led by Vladimir Ilyich Lenin, took over.

Early Communists hoped to take over the entire world by force, which was one reason Germany wanted to crush the Soviets. It's also why France and Great Britain didn't trust Stalin in the late 1930s when he bargained unsuccessfully with them for a defense agreement to protect Russia from Nazi aggression.

In 1991, the Soviet Union disintegrated, splitting into separate countries: Armenia, Azerbaijan, Belarus, Georgia, Kazakhstan, Kyrgyzstan, Russia, Tajikistan, Turkmenistan, Ukraine, and Uzbekistan (all part of the Soviet Union in 1939) and Estonia, Latvia, Lithuania, and Moldova (taken by the Soviets during the Second World War).

Soviet posters

off and an invasion of Great Britain might happen. Tales that Germany now had submarines which could carry 100 soldiers suggested that Germany was about to assault a maritime nation such as Great Britain—certainly not Russia!

A few German military officers even enjoyed a night out while they subtly circulated falsehoods, visiting clubs run by the Nazis for foreign correspondents and dignitaries. Puffing on Dutch cigars, they casually asked the journalists and celebrities questions, obviously preoccupied with gathering information about England, not Russia. One officer pretended to be drunk and declared he even knew the date of the invasion of England. The next day, it was rumored that the Nazis had arrested the officer for revealing military secrets.

For added believability, a newspaper article written by Joseph Goebbels, Germany's propaganda minister, suggested an invasion of Britain would happen soon. It quickly disappeared from newsstands—you guessed it—hastily withdrawn to make it appear the Nazis had suppressed the article.

Winston Churchill, Great Britain's prime minister, wasn't fooled. He had information decoded from German messages. In April 1941, Churchill sent a personal message to Stalin to warn him that German troops were about to attack the Soviet Union. But Stalin didn't believe it. He questioned British motives. He thought they were trying to trick him into declaring war on Germany to help the Allies.

On June 21, 1941—a month later than originally planned—Germany declared war on Russia. The next day, 3 million German soldiers and 3,000 tanks crossed the Russian border. So much for the Nazi-Soviet Pact signed less than two years earlier!

MAN OF STEEL

Joseph Stalin was leader of the Soviet Union from 1929 to 1953. He transformed what had been an undeveloped nation into a world power, but his people paid dearly for progress. Stalin ruled by terror. He exiled, imprisoned, or executed anyone who opposed his decisions, including friends and colleagues who had helped him become leader. Stalin is widely believed to have been responsible for the deaths of 20 million Soviet citizens.

Born in 1879, Stalin grew up in poverty. His mother wanted her intelligent only child to become a priest and sent him to a small church school. He was a good student, but his teachers repeatedly punished him for reading forbidden books on revolutionary social ideas such as Marxism, which he thought would improve the lives of farmers and factory workers. (See Soviet Union, page 26.)

In his late teens, Stalin joined a Marxist group. His school expelled him soon after. In 1901, he began to write for a Marxist newspaper. Using various false names, he organized workers' strikes and set up a secret press. Between 1903 and 1913, government authorities imprisoned him several times for his subversive views. Each time, he escaped.

In 1913, he changed his last name from Dzhugashvili to Stalin, which comes from a Russian word meaning "man of steel." In

A Russian poster of Joseph Stalin

spite of his name change, the government caught up with him and sent him to Siberia, where he stayed until Russian peasants and workers overthrew the government in 1917. When the Marxists emerged as the winners of the Revolution in 1920, Stalin took over as commissar of nationalities. By 1929, he had assumed the powers of a dictator.

During the 1930s, the Russian government took control of all farms and industry, and Stalin severely punished millions of workers and their families who resisted. In 1935, he began executing anyone who might threaten his power, including many of his highest-ranking military officers. As a result, when Hitler invaded in 1941, the Soviets had few experienced officers. The Russian military also lacked up-to-date weapons and equipment. Instead of improving the country's armies, the Soviets had concentrated their efforts on modernizing Russia's industries and agriculture.

Stalin died in 1953. Under his leadership, the Soviet Union had changed from an undeveloped nation into an industrial and military power. Some Russians admired him for his modernization of their country, but many more feared and despised him because he had killed or imprisoned anyone who opposed him.

Stalin (right) talks to his foreign minister, Vyacheslav Molotov (left)

Adolf Hitler

ADOLF HITLER

Adolf Hitler was one of the most destructive conquerors the world has ever known. He had a genius for making speeches and manipulating people, skills he used to become Germany's leader in 1933.

In 1919, Hitler had joined the German Workers' Party. Its members claimed that the government had given away their country's greatness—land and the right to build a military—when a defeated Germany signed the Treaty of Versailles at the end of the First World War.

The party changed its name to the National Socialist German Workers' Party, or Nazi Party for short, and Hitler rapidly took control. His speeches convinced crowds of unemployed Germans to support the Nazi plan for a centralized government headed by a leader with absolute power. Once elected chancellor, Hitler used propaganda and terror to maintain his position, and persecuted those he considered undesirable, such as Communists, Jews, Gypsies, and the disabled.

Hitler also began building Germany's military. He then embarked on an aggressive campaign to expand Germany itself.

In 1938, German forces occupied Austria and made it a part of Germany. The same year, Hitler forced Czechoslovakia to hand over land settled by Germans, later conquering the entire country. The next year, his armies invaded Poland.

It was becoming clear that Hitler wanted most of Europe. A string of brutal invasions followed—including Norway, the Netherlands, and France in 1940, Yugoslavia and the Soviet Union in 1941. Throughout the war, death camps were built and millions were murdered. (See The Holocaust, page 77.)

Meanwhile, Hitler grew more powerful at home. By 1941, he was the head of the German military and directed strategy on each of Germany's fronts. However, Hitler's early military successes were followed by more and more mistakes as the Allies began to resist his expansion.

Hitler had his own ideas on how to run the German intelligence services. He divided them into a number of small agencies, which ended up fighting among themselves. While this structure prevented his opponents from using the resources of the intelligence services to overthrow him, it also reduced the effectiveness of the various agencies. This made the Germans more vulnerable to Allied deceptions.

Later in the war, some Germans realized that Hitler was evil, and others believed his actions would destroy Germany. There were attempts on his life, but each one failed. In April 1945, with the war lost, Hitler committed suicide.

OUT OF THE BLUE

ook—over here! From 1943 to 1945, the U.S. navy did all it could to grab the Germans' attention. The more noise and commotion it could make, the better. The navy was launching phantom assaults, drawing Germany's land, sea, and air forces away from real Allied invasions happening elsewhere. Special effects were always on the menu— clever theatrics that Douglas Fairbanks Jr., a well-known Hollywood actor, picked up in Great Britain then took back to America to share with the U.S. navy.

Fairbanks joined the American navy in 1941 and was sent to Great Britain in 1942 to learn all he could about modern naval tactics. He discovered that his old friend Lord Louis Mountbatten was experimenting with sound, exploring it as a possible weapon to improve British odds during amphibious invasions.

Landing British troops from ships onto the beaches of continental Europe was certain to be difficult and bloody. Clearly, the Germans onshore had the edge, with plenty of natural or man-made cover to hide behind as they fired at the Allies advancing in open boats. How could the Allies even the odds? Mountbatten planned to use sound as a diversion, drawing the enemy away from areas where real troops were landing. Hidden in the distance, Mountbatten would project the recorded noise of tanks, landing craft, and soldiers' voices. Sound effects—just like in the movies!

Fairbanks was intrigued by his friend's experiments and asked to join some mock raids being conducted from the British side of the English Channel. With his own eyes, he saw German soldiers across the Channel fall for the sonic ruse. He was sure this tactic would interest the U.S. navy.

In October 1942, Fairbanks was transferred to Virginia Beach, Virginia, where he approached Admiral Kent Hewitt, then supervising the training of naval forces about to be deployed to the Mediterranean. Fairbanks pitched the idea of creating an elite amphibious combat unit proficient in diversion techniques. Yes, the navy was definitely interested! Within six months, 180 officers and 300 enlisted men had volunteered for the new group, nicknamed Beach Jumpers, or BJs for short. They practiced imitating real landing forces with large ships and scores of landing craft—not an easy task when all they actually had were ten 63-foot (19 m) air-sea rescue boats (ARBs) made of plywood.

The strategy, as in many real invasions, was to operate at night or burn fuel to make thick clouds of smoke to hide

NAME GAME

Several different stories explain how the Beach Jumpers got their name. According to one, the title describes the units' swift and effective harassment of enemy-held beaches. A more entertaining story came from Harold Burris-Meyer, Theater and Sound Research Director for the Stevens Institute of Technology. While working on a navy contract to study the effects of sound on men in warfare, Burris-Meyer was asked the purpose of the newly formed units' work. He answered by saying, "To scare the bejesus out of the enemy." After that, his team referred to the subject of their study as the "BJ factor," which led to the cover name Beach Jumpers.

LORD LOUIS MOUNTBATTEN

Lord Mountbatten, a member of the British royal family, entered the Royal Naval College at the age of 13 and rose to become Supreme Allied Commander in Southeast Asia.

USS *ENDICOTT*

The USS *Endicott* (DD-495), a Gleaves-class
destroyer
LENGTH: 348.33 feet (104.5 m)
BEAM: 36 feet (10.8 m)
DRAFT: 19 feet (5.7 m)
MAXIMUM SPEED: 36.5 knots
CREW: 250

ARMAMENT:
   4 x 5" guns (in single mounts)
   4 x 40 mm Bofors anti-aircraft guns (in twin mounts)
   7 x 20 mm Oerlikon anti-aircraft guns
   5 x 21" torpedo tubes (in a quintuple mount)

The USS *Endicott* was built in Seattle by the Seattle-Tacoma
S.B. Corporation. Laid down May 1, 1941, launched April 5,
1942, commissioned February 25, 1943.

behind. The BJs didn't want enemy soldiers to see the ARBs, each with its giant speaker projecting recorded sounds of ships' engines, landing craft being lowered, and other noises of disembarkation. Also hidden were the radio and radar jammers that some BJs would use to distract enemy radar operators onshore. Axis soldiers would see blips on their radar screens, illusions produced by balloons containing radar reflectors, rockets filled with metal strips, and boats whose dimensions were amplified by an electronic device called Moonshine. When Moonshine detected enemy radar waves, it generated a larger pulse. The enemy received the larger pulse and the genuine reflection at the same time, which gave the impression that the target was much larger than it really was. To top off the effect, "gooney birds"—inflatable dummies—were floated in the water. In poor light, they looked like the torsos of assault troops.

Not everything aboard the ARBs was for creating visual and sound effects, however. They were also equipped with twin .50-caliber machine guns. After all, this was war, not the movies!

By July 1943, the first Beach Jumper Unit (BJU-1) was ready to test its new methods. The Allies were about to invade Sicily, a large island just two miles (3 km) off the southwestern coast of Italy. (See Allied Invasion of Sicily, page 10.) BJU-1's mission was to make the Germans and Italians think that part of the assault would occur at Cape San Marco on the island's southwestern coast, while the real amphibious attack was happening 100 miles (160 km) away. BJU-1 hoped Italian and German troops would rush to Cape San Marco to fend off the Allies, leaving Axis troops at the actual attack shorthanded.

A mile off the cape on the first night of their mock invasion, BJs aboard one ARB unleashed their smoke and sound effects as other BJs prepared their ARBs to sweep parallel to the beach. Suddenly a searchlight onshore scanned the area. The enemy knew they were there. Great! The Germans fired off small arms and artillery. The Americans responded with their guns and rockets, then returned to their home port.

The next night, BJU-1 conducted another operation on the cape, this time with as many ARBs as possible. As a result, an entire German division was kept in reserve. Instead of fighting off the real invasion, many German troops were lying in wait for a phony one.

Missions in Europe and Asia were next. In August 1944, BJU-1, -3, and -5 distracted the enemy as amphibious forces attacked the Germans occupying southern France. Although

ABOVE BOARD

The BJs did more than play tricks. They also carried out beach reconnaissance, recovered downed pilots, rescued secret agents, and supported POW escape lines.

The BJs disbanded at the end of the Second World War. Two units were reactivated in the 1950s when Western and Communist countries fought each other with spies, propaganda, and deception instead of guns. Beach Jumpers also served in the Vietnam War (1965–73). Since 1987, the Beach Jumpers have been known as Fleet Tactical Deception Groups Atlantic and Pacific.

CALIBER: *the width of the bullet a gun fires. A .50-caliber gun fires bullets a half-inch wide.*

THE ASIAN-EUROPEAN CONNECTION

On December 7, 1941, the Japanese attacked the U.S. fleet at Pearl Harbor, Hawaii. They also dropped bombs on British-controlled cities such as Hong Kong and Singapore. The Americans and British declared war on Japan the next day.

Although the United States had declared war only on Japan, it was drawn into the rest of the conflict as well. In 1940, Germany, Japan, and Italy had signed a pact promising to defend one another. The Tripartite Pact forced Germany and Italy to declare war on the U.S. on December 11.

The Allies (the British, Americans, Canadians, and many others) decided that they first had to defeat the Axis in Europe (Germany, Italy, and later others), then attack the Axis in Asia (the Japanese). See world map on page 4.

Top: Douglas Fairbanks Jr. (top left) with the captain of the USS Endicott (top right), shortly after the battle against the German corvettes

Bottom: An air-sea rescue boat (ARB), like those used by the Beach Jumpers

SHIP LENGTH COMPARISON:

BJ boat (ARB) 64 feet/19.2 m

Capriolo (corvette) 215 feet/64.4 m

Aphis (gunboat) 241 feet/72.4 m

USS Endicott (destroyer) 348 feet/104.5 m

most BJ operations received little outside support, this one was covered by two British gunships, the *Aphis* and *Scarab*. Good thing, too, because the operation attracted the attention of two German corvettes (armed escort ships, smaller than destroyers).

Just before dawn two days after the Allied invasion near Saint-Tropez, BJs were returning in ARBs to the USS *Endicott* after a night mission. Suddenly their radar detected two contacts about 1,500 yards (1,350 m) away. The commander of the lead ARB assumed they were British motor launches … until the contacts fired star shells into the sky to illuminate the area. They were German corvettes!

The ARBs sped along zigzag courses as their crews burned fuel to envelop themselves in smoke. Meanwhile, they radioed for help. The *Aphis* and *Scarab* had seen the flares and received the radio message. The gunboats—Fairbanks was aboard the *Aphis*—raced at maximum speed to help. Just before 6 a.m., the gunships opened fire on the corvettes. The enemy shot back, destroying both gunships' radio antennas and gunsights. The gunships also lost electrical power, which meant the crews had to operate the guns by hand. The Allies were losing. After 20 minutes of battle, Fairbanks ordered the gunboats to burn smoke and speed away from the corvettes.

But the Allies hadn't lost yet. Minutes later, the *Endicott* appeared and fired on the corvettes. As the *Endicott* moved in, the corvettes fled. The *Endicott* chased them. Suddenly one corvette, the *Capriolo*, was on fire. Then it exploded! The other corvette, the *Nimet Allah*, capsized.

The two corvettes had been sent to intercept what the Germans thought was an invasion convoy. The corvettes lost 45 men, but the *Endicott*, *Aphis*, and *Scarab* rescued the remaining 211 enemy crew. Incredibly, only three Beach Jumpers were wounded. None died.

Although all BJ missions were dangerous, this one was exceptionally so. For their efforts during the amphibious assault on southern France, the Beach Jumpers earned the Presidential Unit Citation.

Promoted to captain by the end of the war, Douglas Fairbanks Jr. had proven he was more than just a handsome Hollywood actor. For planning successful diversion-deception operations in Europe and Asia, as well as for his part in the invasion of southern France, he was awarded the U.S. Navy Legion of Merit with bronze V (for valor).

HOME INVASIONS

Sefton Delmer and his gang were sly characters. During the Second World War, they sneaked into German submarines, soldiers' huts, officers' quarters, and thousands of civilian living rooms, looking for chances to create mayhem. The Nazis could hear the troublemakers, but they couldn't see them. The enemy's voice had traveled over the airwaves and slipped in via radios.

Delmer had the advantage: he knew Germany well. He had lived in Germany until he was a young teen, the son of an Australian professor who lectured in English at Berlin University. Shortly after graduating from a British university, he worked briefly as a newspaper writer. Then, in 1928, Delmer was hired by the London *Daily Express* to head its Berlin bureau. During his five-year stint in Germany, he met Adolf Hitler and even traveled with him on his private aircraft during the 1932 German general election. Talk about inside knowledge! In fact, for a while his relationship with Hitler looked so cozy that the British government suspected Delmer was in league with the Nazis.

After Berlin, Delmer served as chief European reporter for the *Daily Express* and later headed the newspaper's Paris bureau. When France fell to the German army in 1940, Delmer fled to England, where not only his size—he weighed more than 240 pounds (110 kg)—but his talent for producing effective black propaganda made a big impression on the Political Warfare Executive (PWE). (See Propaganda, page 35.) His true genius emerged when the PWE asked him to organize Gustav Siegfried Eins (GS1), a broadcast station that pretended to be a group inside Germany who opposed the Nazi

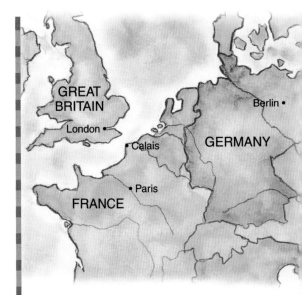

GREAT BRITAIN

London •

• Calais

• Paris

FRANCE

Berlin •

GERMANY

GESTAPO: *Nazi secret police*

German troops relax at their camp by listening to a program on the radio

government. The ruse was sure to waste the Gestapo's time, as they would spend thousands of hours searching Germany for the rebel broadcasters, who were actually in a village in southern England.

GS1's news was always as up-to-date as possible. It was gathered from real German radio shows, smuggled German newspapers, pre-war guidebooks, newly arrived prisoners at British POW camps, and—believe it or not—some incredibly accurate guesses. One July 1942 news item claimed that on October 1, German authorities would require families living in large homes to either move out or take in extra people. According to Der Chef, the radio host, the Nazis would turn seized residences into offices. (Der Chef was trying to make the German people think the Nazis would have more than their share of space while ordinary citizens lived in crowded quarters.) Part of Der Chef's guess was right, although the Nazis gave the order one month later than GS1 had predicted. On November 1, the Nazis began forcing some Germans to share their homes, but not for the reasons Der Chef had claimed; they wanted the space for unfortunate Germans whose homes had been destroyed by Allied bombs. In fact, the Nazis had already begun converting many of their offices back into residences.

Another way Der Chef made his radio show sound authentically German was by making fun of British prime minister Winston Churchill, describing him as flat-footed and drunken. Furthermore, Der Chef grumbled that German aircraft should drop even more bombs on London.

Once Der Chef gained his audience's trust, he craftily spread dissent and despair. If he could lower his listeners' morale, the German people might want to end the war and soldiers might desert the German forces. One fake news story claimed that the occupied French government was sending diseased workers into Germany to spread infection. According to another false story, deaths caused by an illness in children's evacuation camps had dropped from 548 to 372 a month, both numbers guaranteed to dishearten German parents.

In February 1943, Delmer organized another black propaganda station, Atlantiksender, aimed at U-boats

The RAF dropped newspaper-like leaflets called Luftpost *over Germany. This cartoon, in which Hitler appears more than willing to sacrifice German lives, is taken from a July 1941 edition.*

> **TELEPRINTER:** *a machine that sends and receives signals over telephone lines, printing them into readable copy at the receiving end*

PROPAGANDA

Propaganda is a campaign designed to either help or damage a cause by affecting minds and emotions. Some of the most effective wartime propaganda drove a wedge between the group's leaders and its members.

White propaganda came from an acknowledged source like BBC radio, which delivered honest reports that emphasized positive news, such as victories. It made no attempt to disguise its origins.

Gray propaganda came from an undisclosed source. The Allies did not openly declare they were broadcasting Soldatensender Calais, although the American jazz it played, which was not allowed in Germany, was a strong hint.

Black propaganda claimed to come from a different source than it actually did, such as GS1 pretending to be a German radio station.

UNRATIONIERTE WARE

ASPIDISTRA

Aspidistra was a huge transmitter located in Ashdown Forest, as close to the southern coast of England as possible. It was housed underground in a hole excavated by members of a Canadian army road-building unit. The hole was covered with concrete four feet (1.2 m) thick, strong enough to withstand a 1,000-pound (454 kg) bomb.

Aspidistra was sometimes used to hijack real German frequencies when Allied bombers flew into Germany. When German transmitters went off the air to avoid acting as beacons for Allied raiders, regional frequencies closed down with them. But not for long! Aspidistra took over within one two-hundredth of a second, so quickly that listeners couldn't tell that the program was now coming from another source, courtesy of the British. Once a smooth transition had been made, Delmer's cohorts interrupted the program with a special announcement guaranteed to create chaos, such as a report of traffic jams caused by civilians trying to evacuate before Allied bombers destroyed their homes. Shortly after the announcement was finished, Aspidistra relayed a few more minutes of the real German program, then faded away.

Of course, the Nazis were furious! As soon as they recognized a British transmission, they'd announce: "The enemy is broadcasting counterfeit instructions on our frequencies. Do not be misled by them." But the British were not easily censored! They interrupted the German transmissions to claim that the Germans were the counterfeit broadcasters, then continued on with their carefully prepared propaganda.

PROPAGANDA BALLOONS

The British used hydrogen balloons to send propaganda leaflets to Europe. The Balloon Unit could launch 200 balloons in one night, but the wind was favorable only a quarter of the time. Only 60 percent would reach Germany; some even landed back in Britain.

(German submarines). The station mimicked German armed forces radio, providing a mix of news and music, but to hold its audience's attention the British station played better music. One of Atlantiksender's ploys was to play the latest German tunes, secretly flown into Britain from Sweden. But Delmer's best trick was using *hellschreiber*, a teleprinter designed for the German news service and abandoned in London when war broke out. Hooked into the German news network, Atlantiksender obtained news simultaneously with German stations. As you can imagine, this presented Delmer with unlimited opportunities to create mischief, mixing some fiction in with the truth.

When Delmer was ready to work on a more ambitious project in October 1943—radio broadcasts to the German army—GS1 went out with a bang. Shocked listeners heard the Gestapo burst in and shoot Der Chef! Unfortunately, the sound engineer, following normal procedure, replayed the fake shooting later on that day. Oops! The announcer was assassinated twice.

Just a few days after GS1 went off the air, Delmer added another show to his repertoire: Soldatensender Calais (German forces radio, supposedly broadcast from Calais). Although it was aimed at the German army and air force, civilians listened to it too because Aspidistra, a powerful British transmitter, could reach Germany. Soldatensender staff worked diligently to air the news slightly faster than real German radio, gaining the station a reputation for offering the best coverage. Delmer's news was a clever blend of truth and falsehood, such as the claim that a German major general had defected when actually he had been captured. Soldatensender announcers also declared how outraged they were at German soldiers who applied for compassionate leave or faked an injury and then escaped to neutral territory. Of course, the story contained details that disgruntled soldiers could copy.

Even after Soldatensender's cover was blown, the German military were spooked by the British ability to invent believable propaganda. Officers forbade enlisted men to listen to it, but German radio signals in western Europe were less powerful than Aspidistra's. So Soldatensender, as well as Atlantiksender, tempted German listeners—including officers—to tune in right up until April 30, 1945, when the stations finally shut down.

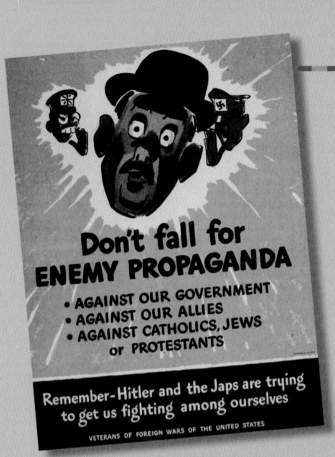

PAPER WAR

Some Allied black propaganda was printed then dropped from aircraft or distributed by hand. One famous trick was to drop forged passes over the German front lines; soldiers could simply sign them, then head for home. Another wily maneuver was to distribute books—disguised as texts such as *Pocket Guide to Oslo* or *The Soldier's Songbook*—that told soldiers how to fake illnesses or slack off. The Allies also created a modified version of a German army medical pamphlet. In it, they listed a variety of minor symptoms as life-threatening, hoping to convince relatively healthy soldiers that they were dangerously ill.

Nachrichten für die Truppen (News for the Troops), a daily newspaper produced by the Allies for German troops, mixed false items with real news. Among the stories were tales of Nazi officials faking their own deaths and heading for neutral territory. They also printed maps showing German units surrounded by Allied forces.

The Allies played paper tricks on German civilians too, supplying fake ration books to drain German cities of supplies.

A poster produced by the Office of War Information, instructing Americans to ignore enemy propaganda

A fake German ration card, produced by the Allies and dropped over Germany. Its producers hoped that people would use the cards to get extra food, leading to a shortage.

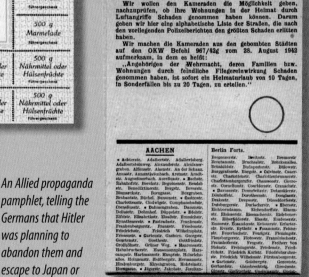

A list of streets in Germany that had been bombed, produced by the British but supposedly created by the Red-Circle resistance group in Germany. It told German soldiers that they had the right to visit their home if it was bombed, hoping to draw troops away from the front lines.

An Allied propaganda pamphlet, telling the Germans that Hitler was planning to abandon them and escape to Japan or Argentina

OPERATION OVERLORD: THE D-DAY LANDINGS

U.S. troops wade from their landing craft to the beach on D-Day

German beach obstacles were designed to rip the bottoms out of Allied landing craft. These, seen at low tide, were placed on a Normandy beach.

The Allied invasion of Normandy was a long time coming: four years, to be exact. Allied planners began plotting the return to mainland Europe soon after the Germans forced the British to withdraw from France at Dunkirk in 1940. The retreat proved to the British that they were not ready to fight the mighty Germans on European soil. They needed to build their strength and formulate a well-thought-out plan.

When the Americans joined the war in December 1941, they argued for a bold attack on northern France. They wanted to strike the Germans head-on. But British prime minister Churchill warned them that if the Allies moved before their soldiers and machinery were ready, French beaches might be "choked with the bodies of the flower of American and British manhood." The Americans conceded. Instead of attacking France, British and American soldiers struck western North Africa, where opposition was weaker.

Waiting for the British and Americans to get ready was hard on

THE FIVE D-DAY BEACHES

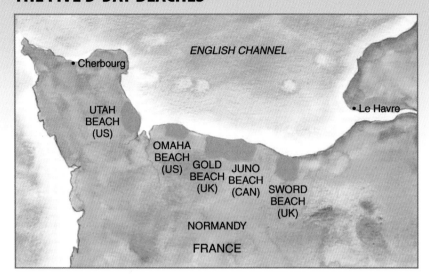

Six divisions landed on five beaches, code-named Utah, Omaha, Gold, Juno, and Sword.

Utah Beach: U.S. 4th Division
Omaha Beach: U.S. 29th and 1st Divisions
Gold Beach: British 50th Division
Juno Beach: Canadian 3rd Division
Sword Beach: British 3rd Division

the Soviet Union. Its leader, Stalin, wanted the Allies to fight along a second front in Europe to draw some German troops from the eastern front, where the Russians were suffering millions of casualties. (See Eastern Front, page 23.) At the Allies' Tehran Conference, attended by Joseph Stalin, Franklin Roosevelt, and Winston Churchill in November 1943, Russia and the United States demanded a firm date for the cross-Channel invasion. Operation Overlord was finally set for May or June 1944.

Now that the Allies had decided on a date for the landing, they needed to choose the site. The Allies needed firm, flat beaches, preferably close to ports and a good network of roads leading into Europe. They also wanted to land within range of fighter aircraft based in southern England, so fighters and bombers could help protect the troops as they landed. Two areas were suitable: the Pas de Calais and Normandy. The Pas de Calais was closer to England, but German defenses were strongest there.

The Allies had good reason to feel anxious about the enemy's defenses. In 1941, the Germans had begun constructing the Atlantic Wall, fortifications along the Atlantic coast of France. They were sturdy forts, built with more

than 17 million tons of concrete and 1.2 million tons of steel. The beach fortifications were armed with machine guns and artillery for sweeping the beaches with gunfire. The Germans had also covered the shoreline below the high-water mark with steel underwater obstacles intended to rip the bottoms out of landing craft heading for the beaches. In addition, they had planted more than 4 million mines on the waterfront, in three separate belts.

Nevertheless, the German military leader, the dreaded Desert Fox, Field Marshal Erwin Rommel (see War in the Western Desert, page 18), wanted even more defenses. He ordered his troops to create another death trap by opening dikes and floodgates to submerge the fields along the coast. He reasoned that paratroopers would drown as they dropped into them. To demolish gliders, he had his men plant "Rommel's asparagus," booby-trapped wooden spikes in suitable fields.

To make matters even worse for the Allies, 41 Axis divisions were waiting in northern France. Nine of them were armored and could strike swiftly to crush the Allies.

Clearly, the Allies needed a seasoned commander to face such a formidable foe. They chose General Dwight D. Eisenhower. He had

ON THE BEACHES

British and Canadian troops stormed Gold, Juno, and Sword beaches with a minimum of difficulty. The Americans met less resistance than anticipated at Utah Beach. The lead troops landed in the wrong area, which turned out to be more lightly defended than the original target area. On the other hand, Americans landing on Omaha Beach suffered heavy losses. German artillery perched on high cliffs rained shells down on them, causing a massive 2,500 casualties.

> **PARATROOPER: a soldier trained and equipped to jump from an aircraft with a parachute into a battle area**

> **BEACHHEAD: a foothold on an enemy-held coast that allows a buildup for further advancement into hostile territory**

successfully commanded the Allied invasions of North Africa, Sicily, and mainland Italy, and had proven to be a good diplomat in keeping the British and American teams working smoothly together. He was also an American, and the majority of troops crossing the Channel would be from the United States.

Even though the Germans appeared to have the advantage, they too faced a huge challenge. They needed to win; there would be no second chance. If the Germans failed to halt the invasion, the Allies would eventually free Europe. But if the Germans crushed the assault, it would take a year or more for the western Allies to gather enough strength to attack again. During that time, the Germans could move the bulk of their troops now in France to the eastern front to defeat the Russians.

According to the Allied plan, shortly after midnight on the day of the invasion, British paratroopers would land on the eastern flank of the landing area and Americans at the western end. Then, at dawn, the largest armada in history would land American, British, and Canadian troops on five beaches. (Four more divisions would land within the next 24 hours.) The British and Canadians would drive towards the city of Caen. South of Caen were flat areas where airfields could refuel Allied fighters. Meanwhile, the Americans would try to cut off the Cotentin Peninsula and the city of Cherbourg, a port.

The next three stories tell how the Allies confused the Germans before and during D-Day about when and where the invasion would take place. Fortitude, the code name for the operation, was the most complicated deception scheme of the entire war. The Allies hoped to gain the edge they needed. If they could surprise the Germans, they might tip the odds in their favor.

PHANTOMS OF THE OPERATION

Crossing the English Channel from England to France looks easy on a map. After all, the distance across the Straits of Dover is only 22 miles (33 km)—the length of 13 Golden Gate Bridges. But what maps don't show is how treacherous the Channel can be. Strong tides, brisk winds, dense fog, and gale-force storms are constant hazards. Nevertheless, the Allies wanted a beachhead on European soil, and the Americans believed crossing the Channel was the best route … even though the Germans were waiting for them on the other side.

By mid-1943, the Allies had defeated the Axis in Africa. Now it was time to battle the Nazis in Europe. Germany controlled most of the continent's coastline except around Spain and Portugal, neutral countries. This meant the Allies had to land on German-occupied territory. As a first step towards weakening the Axis, Prime Minister Churchill of Great Britain favored invading Italy, which he called the "soft underbelly" of Europe. But the Americans insisted that attacking northern France was the better strategy; it was the only way to take the fight to the German homeland. They compromised: the Americans agreed to fight a limited war in Italy, and both nations worked on plans to cross the English Channel.

Of course, the Nazis suspected the Allies' intentions. The shortest distance across the Channel was between Dover and the Pas de Calais. On the French side of the Straits of Dover, the Germans were ready with infantry and panzer divisions, beach obstacles, and huge coastal artillery forts. They could probably defeat the Allies before they even reached the shore!

So the Allies decided to do something unexpected: they'd land at Normandy, which also had suitable harbors and beaches. To trick the enemy into keeping its massive buildup at the Pas de Calais, however, the Allies devised an elaborate strategy called Operation Fortitude South. It was intended to convince the enemy that landings in Normandy were only a diversion. According to the ruse, the Pas de Calais was the true goal.

First, though, the Allies would liberate Norway—another deception, called Operation Fortitude North. Norway? Yes, the Allies wanted to fool the Nazis into believing they would attack German-occupied Norway before they invaded France. They hoped such a lie would cause the Germans

DOUBLE TROUBLE

Many double agents helped the Allies win the Second World War, but two in particular played major roles: Brutus and Garbo. Over the years, both agents passed the Germans "valuable" intelligence, although in reality they only reported information the British wanted the Nazis to know. Reading decoded German messages helped the British pass on lies in line with what the enemy expected to hear. As the Allied invasion of Normandy (D-Day) approached, the Germans trusted Brutus and Garbo to forward accurate intelligence. Their information helped convince the Nazis that the main Allied invasion would happen at the Pas de Calais.

Brutus's real name was Roman Garby-

Continued on page 43

to transfer troops from France to Norway.

To make Operation Fortitude (North and South) look believable, the Allies needed to convince the Germans that something much bigger was brewing than the Allied troop build up across the Channel from Normandy. The Allies needed a phantom army. The challenge was obvious: how to build and maintain the fantasy of non-existent troops. The Germans would surely check every detail!

British intelligence handed the mission to the London Controlling Section (LCS), the nonsense name of a no-nonsense agency that specialized in circulating false information. It was LCS's job to persuade the enemy that the imaginary First United States Army Group (FUSAG) was preparing to cross the Channel at the Pas de Calais. In fact, FUSAG had to seem big enough to detain as many German troops in the Pas de Calais as possible.

For starters, LCS devised a variety of ways to help the Germans discover the "facts." Sometimes, LCS circulated rumors among diplomats from neutral countries with Axis sympathies, such as Spain, hoping they would pass the information on to the Nazis. At other times, LCS "revealed" secrets like unit locations and numbers by placing them in phony marriage and death notices in newspapers. But the most effective way of making sure the Nazis had up-to-date FUSAG information was to tell double agents to include it in their reports.

Luckily, the British had converted more than 40 Nazi spies into double agents—men and women who pretended to spy for one side while actually spying for the other. Many of the double agents were experts at misleading their Nazi controllers with false information, which they claimed to gather from chance conversations with talkative officers or people in bars.

One of the rumors LCS was anxious to spread through its double agents was that General George S. Patton Jr. was scheduled to lead FUSAG. The Germans already respected Patton, who had headed troops in North Africa and Sicily. Next, LCS made up names of commanding officers, and "recruited" units from specific regions in the U.S.

Incredibly, the Heraldic Section of the U.S. War Department tricked *National Geographic*—known for sticking to the truth—into duping the Germans. The army

Czerniawski. He was a Polish air force officer captured by the Germans just after they occupied Poland. The Nazis recruited him to infiltrate Great Britain as a spy, but as soon as he arrived in England, he offered his services to the British. To help persuade the Nazis that the Allies were about to liberate Norway, Brutus told his German contacts he was working for the Polish formations attached to the fictitious Fourth Army in Scotland. He later became a liaison officer with the "headquarters" of the imaginary First United States Army Group (FUSAG) in southeastern England, reporting to his Nazi handlers about the troop buildup and movements of the FUSAG forces.

Garbo—Juan Pujol Garcia—was a Spaniard disenchanted with his government's Nazi sympathies. The British rejected his first offers to work for them, so he decided to sabotage the Nazis on his own. Later, the British hired Garbo when they realized he was so good at storytelling that he might inadvertently hurt their cause if they didn't; some of his lies had been very close to the truth! Garbo became one of the Allies' most successful double agents, certainly one whom Hitler trusted to the very end of the war. Garbo invented a network of 27 imaginary sub-agents. Five of his sub-agents stationed throughout Scotland and Northern Ireland supported Brutus's stories about the fictitious Fourth Army. They also reported that the

Continued on page 44

135th Airborne Division

These fake unit badges were among those featured in National Geographic.

46th Infantry Division

non-existent 52nd Lowland Division had been training in Scotland with mountaineering equipment, which suggested they too were preparing for an attack on Norway.

One of Garbo's greatest moments came on the eve of D-Day. The British realized that, since the Normandy invasion was so massive, at least one of the agents had to send the Nazis an accurate warning. Otherwise, the Germans might suspect that many, or all, of the agents were really working for the Allies. Just hours before the assault—early enough to make the warning sound genuine but too late for the Germans to move their troops in time—Garbo radioed that the attack was about to occur. It worked! The Germans had too little time to send reinforcements to halt the initial invasion of Normandy. What's more, Hitler continued to believe Garbo was faithful to the Nazi cause.

Once the Germans realized the invasion of Normandy was the main operation, Garbo informed his German contacts that the Allies had abandoned the invasion of the Pas de Calais. He added that what remained of FUSAG would join the First Allied Airborne Army for a new large-scale operation—another untruth believed.

helped the magazine's staff prepare a 32-page spread for the June 1943 issue that featured unit insignias, including 21 patches of bogus units.

Meanwhile, physical "proof" of FUSAG's existence began to appear on the English side of the Dover Straits, right across from the Pas de Calais. From the air, it looked real: mock airfields with inflatable rubber tanks and aircraft, harbors filled with dummy landing craft, huge but unoccupied tent encampments, deceptive illumination, and fake radio antennas. To add credibility, a special unit drove up and down England's southern coast broadcasting radio transmissions that sounded like army maneuvers.

The Germans fell for the ruse. By the evening of June 6, 1944 (D-Day), five Allied divisions were ashore at Normandy. Meanwhile, 19 German divisions were still waiting at the Pas de Calais! By the time the Germans realized they had been deceived, it was too late—the Allies had gained a beachhead in Normandy.

German army maps captured later showed that the enemy believed FUSAG was making preparations to attack from southeastern England. The maps also revealed that the Germans believed the division areas and corps headquarters to be exactly where the Allied deception plan had placed them. What's more, the enemy grossly overestimated Allied strength in England, believing there were 79 divisions instead of the actual 52.

GENERAL GEORGE S. PATTON JR.

George S. Patton began his career in the U.S. army as a cavalry officer but switched to tanks as soon as they were introduced during the First World War. He was one of the few American believers in armored warfare, and he proved his point when he commanded the U.S. Seventh Army in the invasion of Sicily (see page 10). His achievements impressed even the Germans.

Patton lost his command when he slapped a hospitalized soldier, calling him a coward. But soon after, the army used his name and reputation to build up FUSAG in the eyes of German intelligence. After the D-Day invasion was over, Patton took command of the U.S. Third Army, racing across France. His troops were first across the Rhine (see page 56). Hard-driving and showy, his profane language was also legendary. While Patton was well known for the pair of pearl-handled pistols he carried around, few knew he had competed in the 1912 Olympics.

TOP PERFORMANCE

The Allies hoped to take Normandy by surprise, but hiding the buildup of troops and military equipment on the British side of the English Channel was impossible. So instead, the Allies decided to deceive the enemy by creating "evidence" that the D-Day attack would happen not only at a different place but also at a different time than actually planned. They wanted the Germans to believe they would land at the Pas de Calais sometime in July 1944, instead of at Normandy in June. (See Phantoms of the Operation, page 41.)

To further confuse the Germans, the British fostered the illusion that another invasion might happen soon, probably in the Balkans or southern France. The Germans were watching for more clues. They were particularly interested in General Sir Bernard Montgomery's whereabouts. As one of Britain's top military leaders, Monty, as he was fondly called, was sure to be part of any major invasion.

That gave the Allies an idea. A former theater critic working on deception plans for the British army remembered a junior officer who closely resembled the famous general—Lieutenant Meyrick Clifton-James. Perhaps Clifton-James could trick the Nazis into believing Montgomery was in North Africa as part of a planned Allied invasion of France's Mediterranean coast. They might also conclude that the cross-Channel assault was still weeks away, reasoning that if it were about to happen, Monty would remain with his troops.

The theater critic knew about Clifton-James because the lieutenant had already played the general at a show put on by an army amateur theater troupe in London. In March, Clifton-James had appeared onstage dressed like Monty, in a greatcoat and beret. The crowd had gone wild with enthusiasm. They cheered and hollered, convinced that the actor was the general himself. The story of the impersonation appeared in the London *News Chronicle*.

Later that spring, Clifton-James received a phone call from the movie actor David Niven, a lieutenant-colonel in the army. Niven said the army wanted Clifton-James to do a screen test for some army films. Clifton-James was pleased. He had been an actor before the war, but the army had placed him in the payroll department. Working on army films sounded much more to his liking.

When Clifton-James reached London, military intelli-

THE ITALIAN FRONT

The Allied invasion of North Africa was going well in January 1943, so the Allies began to plan where they would strike the Axis next. The arguments were heated. The Americans wanted to launch an invasion across the English Channel. The British favored expanding Allied operations in the Mediterranean to capitalize on their successes in North Africa. The Soviet Union just wanted any second European front to divert some Nazi forces from the eastern front. After much debate, the Allies agreed to invade Sicily. (See Dead Ringer, page 10.) Their long-term objectives were to help Russia by pinning down German troops in Sicily and to knock Italy out of the war.

The Allies invaded Sicily in July 1943 and mainland Italy two months later. The German forces in southern Italy withdrew to a strong defensive line in mountainous terrain criss-crossed by rivers. After eleven months of fierce fighting, the Allies entered Rome on June 4, two days before D-Day. North of Rome lay another major defensive line. The Allies pierced it in mid-September, but torrential rains and mud prevented them from going much further. Finally, in April 1945, Allied troops broke through into northern Italy. Historians often debate how useful the Italian campaign was to the Allied cause, but it did tie up a large number of German troops.

gence told him a modified version of the truth: they wanted him to impersonate Monty in Great Britain while the real general went off to launch an invasion from the Mediterranean. The less the actor knew at this point, the less chance the enemy would find out.

For the next few days, Clifton-James studied newspaper photos and watched newsreels of Monty. He drilled for hours to make sure he knew all the details, such as old friends and their nicknames, what Monty did and didn't like, and military protocols (since Clifton-James was a lieutenant, not a general). Next, dressed as a sergeant of the Intelligence Corps, Clifton-James followed Montgomery around for two days. His job was to study the general's gestures: his unique salute (a double motion that looked like a greeting), his walk with his hands clasped behind his back, and his habit of pinching his cheek when he was thinking. He also met with the general to get his voice exactly right. Meanwhile, Monty's tailor made him a copy of the general's uniform.

Although Clifton-James easily mastered Monty's gestures, a missing middle finger on the actor's right hand was a giveaway. Since Monty rarely wore gloves, Clifton-James had to wear an artificial finger made of cotton wool and adhesive. But two of Clifton-James's habits were potentially bigger problems. He was both a smoker and a drinker. Montgomery was neither. The actor would have to be careful; spies could be anywhere.

Once ready to play his part, Clifton-James learned the truth: instead of staying in England while Monty flew to Gibraltar and North Africa, the reverse would take place. Clifton-James would fly to Gibraltar and North Africa, pretending to work on a bogus operation called Plan 303.

On May 25, Clifton-James, dressed as Monty, boarded a plane to Gibraltar. Bad news: he also smuggled on a flask of gin. By the time his co-travelers discovered the gin, he was drunk! His aide, who was part of the deception, had to sober him up fast. The actor was splashed with cold water and flown to a high altitude to make him vomit.

Fortunately, by the time the plane landed in Gibraltar, Clifton-James was feeling well enough to play his role. Gibraltar's governor, General Sir Ralph Eastwood, met "Monty" at the airfield. Eastwood was one of the few people in on the plan because he and the real Monty had attended military academy together, and he would not be fooled by a double.

Eastwood was impressed with Clifton-James's act and assured him his performance was believable. Together they went to a dinner party attended by several Spanish guests, one of whom was known to be an informant for German intelligence. Two hours

A British bomber and crew in front of the Rock of Gibraltar

GIBRALTAR

Gibraltar is a tiny British colony on the southern coast of Spain where the Mediterranean Sea meets the North Atlantic Ocean. During World War II, it was the main British base between Britain and the Middle East, but it was extremely insecure. Abwehr agents with telescopes could observe the British airfield from Spanish territory. Although Spain was officially neutral during the Second World War, Spanish troops fought the Soviet Union alongside the Germans. General Francisco Franco of Spain, like Hitler, was a dictator.

During the Second World War, the British excavated miles of tunnels beneath the Rock (as Gibraltar is known), then built an underground hospital and shops to sell frozen meat, baked goods, and distilled water.

ALGIERS: the capital of Algeria, a French colony during the Second World War

MONTGOMERY OF ALAMEIN

Bernard Law Montgomery was one of the best known and most controversial Allied leaders. Many military officers thought he was insensitive, outspoken, and domineering. But he was popular with his men and a confident, hard-driving strategist with a fine eye for detail.

Monty was born in 1887 in south London but grew up in Tasmania (southeast of Australia). He joined the British army and served as an officer in World War I.

In the summer of 1942, Monty was appointed commander of the Eighth Army in the Western Desert. Beginning with the Battle of El Alamein (see Working Magic, page 18), Monty led his troops in a series of successful battles that proved to the Allies that the Germans could be beaten. The Eighth Army forced the Afrika Korps back to Tunisia, and then invaded Sicily and the rest of Italy.

In December 1943, Monty returned to Great Britain to help plan the Normandy invasion. As commander of the 21st Army Group, he commanded all troops involved in the actual landing. In September 1944 (after D-Day), he was promoted to field marshal.

After the war, he was made a lord, with the title Viscount Montgomery of Alamein. He served as chief of the Imperial General Staff from 1946 to 1948, and finished his career as NATO Deputy Supreme Allied Commander Europe. He died in 1976.

after Eastwood and Clifton-James left the party, the Abwehr in Madrid had the news that Monty was visiting Gibraltar.

The next morning, Clifton-James's plane developed a bogus mechanical problem, which delayed his departure from Gibraltar to North Africa. The actor waited in the airport canteen, where he dropped a handkerchief monogrammed with Monty's initials. The British knew that a canteen employee worked for the Abwehr, so Clifton-James also dropped the phrase "Plan 303."

An honor guard of French colonial troops later greeted Clifton-James in Algiers, where the actor was treated like a hero. A crowd of civilians had gathered to catch a glimpse of the famous general. According to carefully planted rumors, Monty was in North Africa to discuss a possible U.S. and British invasion of southern France.

While the airport greeting was fun, the 12-mile (19 km) car ride from the airport to Algiers was nerve-racking. Gossip had it that someone might attempt to murder Monty. Since no troops could be spared to act as bodyguards, the car sped with sirens blaring all the way into the city. As you can imagine, Clifton-James was relieved when he reached the safety of army headquarters.

For the next few days, Clifton-James attended official receptions, saluted troops lining city streets, waved to crowds of civilian spectators, and dropped subtle hints about Plan 303. Clifton-James's tour had been scheduled so he would not meet officers who knew him personally, unless they were in on the ruse.

A few days before D-Day, his performance was over. Clifton-James changed back into his lieutenant's uniform and the army smuggled him onto a plane for Cairo. He stayed in Egypt until after D-Day, then returned home as Clifton-James.

Sworn to secrecy, Clifton-James returned to his paymaster's job. All the military would let him tell his co-workers was that he had been away to work on army propaganda films. According to his story, the movies were filmed in Africa because they involved secret weapons. But more people tended to believe that the military had detained and questioned him for an offense, possibly espionage. Although Clifton-James could convincingly portray a trustworthy person, in real life he was sometimes undependable.

After the war was over, Clifton-James learned that his performance was one of many deceptions that helped make the invasion of Normandy a surprise and a success.

THREE DOTS AND A DASH

The D-Day invasion had begun. Just after midnight on June 6, 1944, scores of Douglas C-47 cargo planes dropped the first Allied troops behind enemy lines. Thousands of paratroopers landed in Normandy, a province in northwestern France. The paratroopers were the vanguard of a massive assault: the Allies intended to secure a beachhead from which to liberate France and eventually the rest of Nazi-occupied Europe.

At dawn, shiploads of American, British, and Canadian troops would land on five Normandy beaches. The first few hours were critical. The invading troops would be most vulnerable to attack as they approached the shore then advanced across obstacle-strewn beaches covered by German artillery and machine guns. Time was precious. Within hours, German reinforcements could easily crush the invasion. Indeed, the enemy had been lying in wait for months. The Germans knew the assault would come eventually, although they did not know when or where. Now the Allies had to do everything they could to stop enemy reinforcements from reaching Normandy.

In the pre-dawn darkness, the paratroopers—many of them battle-hardened veterans of the Sicilian and Italian campaigns—prepared the way for the soon-to-arrive troops. Some captured key bridges that led to the heart of occupied France. The goal was to seize them before German soldiers could blow them to bits. The Allies would need to cross the bridges as they advanced into Europe. Other paratroopers secured the northeastern and southwestern flanks of the landing area, to protect the troops from an enemy advance as they struggled to reach safer ground.

Further inland, Allied commandos and members of the French resistance dynamited railway signal boxes, switches, and tracks to stop German reinforcements from arriving by train. They also cut power and telephone lines into northwestern France to keep the German high command in Berlin from knowing the details of what was happening for as long as possible. But trains and communications to Normandy were not the only ones shut down; that would give away the location of the invasion. The German higher-ups still believed the Allies would invade the coast along the Pas de Calais, some 200 miles (320 km) to the north of the Normandy beaches. (See Phantoms of the Operation, page 41.) Now the challenge was to keep them from learning the truth.

Sustaining the deception required a complicated

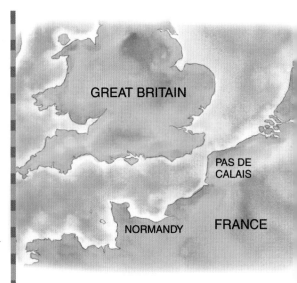

STANDARD PARACHUTIST PACK

Each paratrooper carried approximately 70 pounds (32 kg) of equipment. Each officer averaged 90 pounds (41 kg) of gear. Since they were dropping into unknown territory, they needed to be prepared for many conditions. This is what they took:

- M-1 Garand rifle with eight-round clip
- Cartridge belt with canteen • Flares
- Parachute and pack • Pocket compass
- Anti-flash headgear and gloves
- Machete • .45-caliber Colt pistol
- Message book • Hand grenades

EMERGENCY RATIONS

- 4 pieces chewing gum • 4 chocolate bars
- 2 bouillon cubes • 1 package hard candy
- 1 package pipe tobacco • 2 instant coffees
- 2 sugar cubes and creamers
- 1 bottle water-purifying tablets

VANGUARD: troops who move ahead of the main part of the army

Ike, as Dwight Eisenhower was fondly called, radiated enormous personal charm. People everywhere liked him—although, as a student at West Point, he was often in trouble for playing pranks and disobeying minor school rules. But once he graduated in 1915, he proved to be an excellent trainer of tank battalions and an outstanding strategist.

Soon after the Japanese attacked Pearl Harbor, Hawaii, in December 1941, Ike was appointed head of the War Plans Division of the War Department. The next spring, he argued that the U.S. should concentrate on a cross-Channel attack on German-occupied Europe rather than spread itself thin across many battlefields. But the British believed the Allies weren't ready to launch an attack on the Continent. So, as the Allied nations built up their military strength, Eisenhower directed the Allied forces in successful campaigns in North Africa, Sicily, and Italy.

By spring 1944, the Allies were at last prepared to attack the Germans on European soil. Eisenhower was appointed Supreme Commander of the Allied air, sea, and ground forces. It was his responsibility to decide exactly when Allied troops would invade occupied France, although moonlight, weather, and Channel tides also helped determine the date.

On June 5, the moonlight was bright and the tides were low. Invading soldiers could spot obstacles such as mines the Germans had planted on the beaches. Unfortunately, the weather was terrible: high winds, fog, and choppy seas.

Ike postponed the invasion for 24 hours. Then, forecasters predicted a brief period during which the weather would improve. Ike agonized whether to invade the next day or wait for two weeks, when the moon and tides would again be advantageous. After consulting with his advisers, he decided postponement would break his troops' morale. Even worse, during a two-week wait, word of the invasion could leak to the Germans. So, June 6 it was! As it turned out, although the conditions were not perfect, luck and surprise favored the Allies.

Eisenhower returned to the U.S. a hero. The Americans elected him president in 1952 and 1956. During his two terms, he remained as popular on the home front as he had been on the battlefield. He died in 1969.

scheme made up of many operations. Offshore, northeast of the invasion area, still other Allied troops were crafting illusions to confuse the Germans. Radar experts had discovered ways to fabricate mirages that would appear on German radar screens, making the Germans see what the Allies wanted them to see. The experts had also devised ways to hide events they hoped to keep secret. They used jammers to produce extra radar signals, so that when all the signals reached the enemy's screens, they didn't know which echoes were real. In two separate operations, a total of 24 small ships sailed from Britain towards the Pas de Calais. Each boat trailed a 29-foot (8.7 m) balloon with a 9-foot (2.7 m) radar reflector. On German radar, each balloon looked like a 10,000-ton transport, which could be carrying a thousand troops! Aircraft circled overhead and, every 12 minutes, dropped strips of aluminum foil called Window. On German radar, Window looked like a fleet of ships. Altogether, the balloons and Window appeared to be a massive invasion.

The trick was risky. For it to remain convincing, the planes had to fly in a precise orbit over the boats as they sailed closer to the coast. Only the best squadrons were chosen for this task, and even they had had to practice for hours beforehand. Of course, closer to land the enemy could see how small the boats really were. So, 10 miles (16 km) offshore, the crews concealed their true identity by launching smokescreens. Next, giant loudspeakers broadcasted the recorded clanks, rumblings, and splashes of ships dropping anchor—the sounds a fleet made when it prepared to land troops. The Germans fell for the ploy. Instead of heading for Normandy to attack the real

THE C-47

The Douglas C-47 was the military version of the Douglas DC-3, a twin-engine transport plane that first appeared in 1935. The Douglas Aircraft Company manufactured them in Santa Monica, California. The C-47 featured a reinforced fuselage and strong cabin floors for heavy loads, as well as large doors in the rear fuselage for loading cargo and dropping paratroops. More than 10,000 were manufactured between 1942 and 1945. It had powerful engines and cruised at 155 miles (250 km) per hour, with a range of 1,600 miles (2,560 km). The Allies used C-47s to haul cargo, transport troops, drop paratroopers, and tow gliders. They were used as flying ambulances, too. The C-47 was also called the Dakota or Skytrain.

invaders, they remained in the Pas de Calais to defend that province from the two imaginary armadas.

To add to the confusion, another operation was carried out southwest of the invasion zone. A few commandos and hundreds of rubber dummies parachuted in to distract the enemy from the real attacking paratroopers. The dummies were dressed in uniforms and helmets. They were also equipped with recordings of gunfire and exploding mortar rounds, and when they hit the ground, "pintail bombs" launched flares into the air. As soon as the commandos landed, they added their own special effects, for example by releasing chemicals that smelled like exploding shells. To the Germans, it appeared to be a large airborne drop.

Meanwhile, radar jammers hid the real invasion from German screens as the Allies neared the Normandy shore. At first, when the enemy finally *did* see the real invasion, a few high-ranking German officers discounted it as just another deception!

Sadly, 9,000 to 10,000 Allied lives were lost on D-Day. But overall, the invasion was a success. One of the last C-47s leaving England flashed three dots and a dash—Morse code for V, standing for the victory they hoped for. Approximately 24 hours later, more than 150,000 American, British, and Canadian troops had entered France by air and sea.

In the end, German field marshal Erwin Rommel was right. He was commander of Army Group B, stationed in France to meet the expected Allied invasion. He predicted a few months before D-Day: "The war will be won or lost on the beaches. We'll have only one chance to stop the enemy, and that's while he's in the water, struggling to get ashore."

GHOST OF A CHANCE

Now you see them, now you don't. The American 23rd Headquarters Special Troops, also called the Ghost Army, were master illusionists. Instead of confronting the Axis with guns and artillery, the 23rd used visual and sound effects to defeat the enemy. They were unusual soldiers, mostly actors, architects, artists, designers, meteorologists, and sound technicians. Their mission was to impersonate other troops, replacing them without the enemy noticing that the real troops were gone.

On a typical assignment, the 23rd pretended to be combat troops. While the soldiers they imitated sneaked off to a new position to surprise the enemy. To convince the Germans that nothing had changed, the 23rd swapped real tanks and steel artillery with rubber dummies, inflated on the spot with motor-operated compressor pumps. They kept night fires burning, visited supply dumps, and continued to do whatever the troops they stood in for had done. They were so well briefed that they even chatted with civilians about recent happenings that anyone in the real combat unit would have known about. For added realism, some actors were bandaged and "bloodied" with cosmetics. The ruse had to convince everyone, since anyone—a shopkeeper, a farmer, even a teenager on a bicycle—could be a spy.

Each mission posed its own challenges. In July 1944, approximately 400 Ghost Army troopers replaced the entire 2nd Armored Division in northern France. As trained, the 23rd inflated their rubber artillery and tanks. Cracks and tears in the props were potential problems, but so far the plan appeared to be going smoothly. Then one tank leaked some air and its cannon drooped. No one knows if the Germans noticed the mistake, but the enemy did see the real 2nd Armored Division change its position. Instead of moving out under cover of darkness, the division had left in broad daylight. The Germans certainly kept tabs on where the armored division was going!

By August, the 23rd was more experienced and a lot wiser. The Allies were trying to take Brest, a French port occupied by the Germans. The army ordered the 23rd to simulate a real tank unit to make it appear there were more U.S. troops outside the city than there really were, hoping the enemy would believe they were outnumbered and surrender. In addition to inflated tanks and artillery, the 23rd unleashed special effects to make the Germans

M3 HALF-TRACK

The M3 half-track was an American armored vehicle used to transport soldiers and pull artillery guns. Tracks replaced its rear wheels, allowing it to move faster than a normal truck over rough ground. Each M3 could carry 13 people and had a maximum speed of 40 miles (64 km) per hour.

think they were under fire. Their weapons were actually electrically ignited flash/sound canisters filled with gunpowder, which at night produced a display that looked and sounded genuine.

The 23rd also assaulted the port with amplified recordings of war sounds. Engines roared, gears clashed, and voices shouted orders, counter-orders, and the occasional curse—the usual noise made by tanks and soldiers as they took up and withdrew from positions. The sounds came from huge speakers called junior heaters, mounted on an M3 half-track truck. The 23rd had recorded the sound on a magnetic wire, something like magnetic tape in a cassette. The wire played for 30 minutes, then rewound while a second wire played.

The recordings were amazingly believable. Friendly troops not in on the ruse were fooled. Even better, so were the Germans! But instead of evacuating, the Germans had already decided to stand and fight no matter what. The Allies took Brest weeks later, in mid-September. Although the enemy hadn't surrendered, the 23rd did keep a sizable German force from attacking the combat troops trying to capture the city.

For the next three months, the 23rd continued to trick the Germans as the Allies moved northeastward towards Belgium and Germany. They never wore their own badge and insignia; it would blow their cover if a spy saw them. Instead, they wore the badge of whatever unit they impersonated, hoping spies would take note. In fact, the 23rd had fun making sure the enemy did notice them. One favorite ploy was for a trooper to dress in a general's uniform. His "driver" and "guards" then drove him in a jeep to the nearest town where enemy agents might see them. At other times, artists painted the 23rd's jeeps and trucks with another unit's markings, then troops drove the vehicles in a convoy through a nearby town. Sometimes, the same vehicles went through the town several times to make the convoy seem much larger!

Problems arose, of course. Dummy tanks inflated in the dark were sometimes positioned facing in the wrong direction. This was certain to tip off enemy aerial reconnaissance, which usually flew overhead at first light, before the 23rd could spot their mistake. Hot sun was another issue. Heat weakened the rubber, creating leaks. The 23rd feared that limp gun barrels in the morning would reveal

GHOST ARMY

The 23rd Headquarters Special Troops were divided into four units:

✪ The 244th Signal Company's mission was to develop and use the radio traffic of whatever unit it was impersonating. Trickster radio operators sent realistic-sounding messages. They knew they had fooled the enemy when the Germans tried to use the fake network to confuse the Allies by broadcasting their own false messages on it.

✪ The 3132nd Signal Service Company specialized in sonic deception techniques. They recorded the sounds made by military equipment and vehicles from a range of distances under various weather conditions. The 23rd had a mobile recording studio to capture sounds not already in their library. Noise from their speakers sounded like military operations happening just out of sight. Under cover of night, the 3132nd could trick the Germans into believing an entire armored division was on the move.

✪ The 603rd Engineer Camouflage Battalion built and set up camouflage and dummy equipment. Realistic from a distance, the dummies included tanks, guns, jeeps, trucks, and even light planes—all made from rubber. Just before the bulk of the Allied troops crossed the Rhine River (see Crossing of the Rhine, page 56), the 603rd inflated 618 dummies to simulate the two divisions that had secretly relocated for the assault.

✪ The 406th Engineer Security Company Special (formerly known as Company A of the 293rd Engineer Combat Battalion) was a disciplined fighting unit that provided the 23rd's security and worked on tough construction jobs. Often, the 406th were the only troops protecting the vulnerable deception artists from the enemy.

A pontoon bridge used by the Allies to cross the Rhine River in 1945. Pontoon bridges were temporary bridges that were kept from sinking by the floats underneath them. The bridges came under heavy enemy fire, but even if individual pontoons were destroyed, the bridge would not sink.

CROSSING OF THE RHINE

The Rhine River in Germany was the Allies' last major hurdle as they headed for Berlin to take Germany's capital city.

On March 7, 1945, U.S. troops from the First Army, led by General Omar Bradley, captured a bridge over the Rhine at Remagen. Two weeks later, on March 22, U.S. troops from General George Patton's Third Army also crossed the Rhine. Bradley and Patton could now brag that they had crossed the Rhine before the British. By the next evening, the First and Third consolidated their hold on the east bank.

However, the British 21st Army Group, led by General Bernard Montgomery, made the main Allied assault across the Rhine. During the three days before the crossing, the Allies flew 11,000 bomber raids against the Germans on the other side of the river. Then, on the evening of March 23, 1945, assault troops crossed the river. At the same time, two airborne divisions (the British 6th and the U.S. 17th) landed on the far bank. By nightfall of the next day, the assault troops had linked up with the airborne troops. Their success was the signal for other Allied armies to press forward and take Germany.

the truth about the phony vehicles. Even worse, heat sometimes caused the rubber to expand and explode, ruining the prop.

After nine months of mostly successful performances in Europe, the 23rd played their last gig near Viersen, Germany, in March 1945. The Allies were about to cross the Rhine River, heading towards Hitler's headquarters in Berlin. The U.S. Ninth Army needed to convince the enemy that Allied troops were about to traverse the Rhine near Viersen, whereas they actually planned to cross the river farther north, near the Dutch border.

While one of the Ninth's units quietly moved northward to prepare for the real crossing, the 23rd teamed up with the rest of the Ninth's soldiers. They kept up an elaborate charade, pretending to amass building supplies for a bridge that would be ready sometime in April, judging by the speed the engineers were working. Speakers amplified the sounds of a massive building effort. Troops inflated rubber construction equipment, tanks, and airplanes. Engineers erected temporary buildings, even medical facilities. A "vehicle control center" using radios pretended to direct the heavy traffic of workers driving construction equipment. Meanwhile, troops paraded army vehicles through the streets of Viersen and talkative "drunks" gave away "secret strategies" in bars.

On March 24, under cover of darkness, the rest of the Ninth sneaked northward and crossed the Rhine. The Germans were shocked. Their intelligence sources had been duped!

To reward a job well done, the Ninth Army's commander presented the 23rd with a commendation for "careful planning, minute attention to detail, and diligent execution." But back home, few people had heard of the Ghost Army's artful deceptions: until 1996, the U.S. army classified their activities "top secret."

RESISTANCE

Resistance fighters had to be brave. Capture during the Second World War usually meant torture and death. Despite this, resistance fighters dared to try to free their countries from Nazi or Japanese control.

Throughout German-occupied Europe, the resistance—mostly civilians—cut telephone, telegraph, and electrical lines. They also blew up bridges, roads, and railway equipment to slow down enemy movement. In addition, they sabotaged factories that manufactured war materials for the Nazis. Instead of using tanks and heavy artillery, resistance fighters relied on their wits to survive and strive to inflict maximum damage.

Fear for their lives did not stop the Oslo Gang. In broad daylight, they boldly hijacked a delivery truck filled with ration cards. The danger was worth it: the successful raid helped keep young Norwegian men from being forced to fight for the Germans on the eastern front.

Belorussian peasants fought long and hard to defeat the Nazis. At first, they had few weapons and no training. But they were resourceful. They scrounged guns, grenades, and mines left behind by retreating Russian troops when the Germans first invaded the Soviet Union. They sabotaged trains and trucks supplying enemy troops with food, fuel, and ammunition.

Coastwatchers Jack Read and Paul Mason were courageous too. From their hideaway jungle huts on the Solomon Islands, they had perfect views of Japanese aircraft flying to Guadalcanal, an island to their south. If they could radio what they saw in time, they hoped to help the Americans secure a strategic base on the island.

But resistance movements were not always successful. The Nazis controlled the Dutch resistance for more than a year. Unaware of what had happened, the British kept parachuting more agents in to be met by Germans who then captured, tortured, and murdered them.

Many courageous people endangered their lives to help the military defeat the enemy.

This portable printing press was used by the French resistance to create false documents for its agents. The document above was produced by the Polish resistance.

PREP SCHOOL

Death-defying stunts, high-tech gadgets, and magnificent vehicles: a secret agent's life is glamorous and thrilling … if you believe the movies. Real-life operatives did face incredibly dangerous situations, but few drove fancy cars or attended luxurious parties.

In fact, most agents hired by Britain's Special Operations Executive (SOE) were ordinary citizens—schoolteachers, art students, even hairdresser's assistants. They joined the SOE to help the people of occupied Europe fight the Nazis. Some worked as radio operators. Others helped organize and equip local resistance groups, committed sabotage, and created mayhem.

Not everyone who applied was accepted. Each applicant had to pass a series of interviews then attend a special school. The SOE needed to be certain that every candidate was right for the job.

The SOE was a secret, so most candidates initially believed they had applied to become interpreters. They all spoke at least one language other than English. Some had answered newspaper ads, though many were actively recruited because someone at SOE believed they were good prospects. Each applicant faced an interviewer in a stark hotel room furnished with only a desk and two chairs. For 40 to 50 minutes, the candidate answered questions to prove he or she could speak a foreign language well enough to blend in with the citizens of a German-occupied country.

Next, British intelligence investigated the background of everyone who passed the language test. At a second interview, SOE told trustworthy candidates some of the truth: the job risked possible capture, torture, and death. Of course, the SOE didn't expect applicants to accept right away, but let them think about it for a few days.

Applicants who were still interested progressed to Preliminary School. Instructors watched students closely to judge their character during four weeks of physical training, weapons handling, unarmed combat, elementary demolitions, map reading, and basic radio communications. Most students still didn't know what their job would be, although the classes in combat and demolitions were certainly clues. Secrecy was still important. Not everyone passed. SOE sent anyone who didn't to the "cooler," a detention site at Inverlair in the Scottish Highlands, where they stayed until their knowledge of the organization

SPECIAL OPERATIONS EXECUTIVE

By early summer 1940, Germany had occupied most of western Europe. In July, Great Britain's prime minister, Winston Churchill, established the Special Operations Executive (SOE), which was formed, he said, to "set Europe ablaze." SOE supported resistance movements. It helped them gather intelligence, amass weapons, plan sabotage, and build escape lines. More than 100 SOE agents did not survive the war. In fact, 13 of the 39 women sent to France were executed in concentration camps.

Perhaps SOE's greatest achievements occurred in France just before, during, and after the D-Day landings. (See Operation Overlord, page 38.) U.S. general Dwight Eisenhower said the SOE and the French resistance were worth five extra divisions because they had helped prevent German reinforcements from reaching Normandy. (See Danger Ahead, page 81.)

> **PARAMILITARY: civilian group that acts like a military organization**

A sign at the entrance to Camp X, SOE's training center in Canada. Camp X trained agents for the Royal Canadian Mounted Police, the American FBI, and the U.S. Office of Strategic Services, as well as SOE.

23-YEAR-OLD HERO

Only five feet (1.5 m) tall, Violette Szabo proved she could keep up with the best SOE agents in France.

Szabo's French mother and English father met in France during the First World War. Szabo spent most of her childhood in England. After graduating from school, she worked as a hairdresser's assistant and then as a sales assistant in a department store. Her life took a dramatic twist when she met and married a captain in the Free French forces in England. (See page 82.) The Nazis had just occupied France, and soon her husband, Étienne, was posted to North Africa. He died in battle a few months after the birth of their daughter, Tania.

The SOE recruited Szabo, who was eager to do all she could to help the French resistance. The Nazis had recently arrested many resistance fighters in northwest France. In April 1944, Szabo parachuted in to find out how strong and trustworthy the resistance movement was near the city of Rouen. Nazi spies had indeed infiltrated some groups. The Nazis arrested her twice, but both times she talked her way out of trouble. Mission accomplished, she went home to England.

In June, the SOE sent Szabo into France again. This time, a German patrol ambushed her. She endured weeks of brutal interrogation but told her captors nothing. Police sent her to a concentration camp, where she was executed a few months later. She was only 23 years old.

After her death, King George VI of Great Britain presented the George Cross to Szabo's four-year-old daughter, and France awarded Szabo the Croix de Guerre.

could no longer help the enemy. Some stayed there until the end of the war.

The graduates went to paramilitary schools (also called Group A) for three to five weeks. Group A was based at remote hunting lodges near Arisaig in northern Scotland. Security was tight.

A hike over difficult terrain evaluated the would-be agents' physical fitness as well as map- and compass-reading skills. Students trudged up mountains, bushwhacked through under-brush, and crawled on their bellies—a trek that guaranteed cuts and bruises. For some, it was probably a relief to spend time later in a classroom studying elementary Morse code!

During other classes, pupils practiced shooting handguns, aiming at a moving, life-sized target on a winch that sped towards them at lifelike speed. SOE also trained them in raid tactics, demolition, and explosives. By the time they used dummy explosives to "blow up" a train supplied by the West Highland Line, the candidates knew for sure that their future job involved sabotage.

Next, students discovered how they, like most SOE operatives, would sneak into occupied Europe: by parachute. They trained at Ringway (now Manchester Airport) for two weeks. Each student had to make at least two jumps, one from a plane and one from a balloon. Strapped to one leg of each trainee as he or she practiced was a little spade, used to bury the chute and jumpsuit after landing. To avoid radar detection, agents had to jump from only 300 to 400 feet (90 to 120 m). That's barely long enough for a chute to open! Some agents broke bones when they landed.

One in three students failed Group A, and—you guessed it—they joined those in the cooler at Inverlair who hadn't passed Preliminary School.

Students who passed Group A went on to Group B, moving to Beaulieu House in southern England, where they prepared for their secret lives in occupied Europe. SOE gave each a cover story to help the agent blend into his or her future environment. Would-be agents learned how to disguise themselves quickly by wearing glasses, parting their hair differently, or walking with an altered gait. Other classes offered hints on how to recognize the enemy, such as watching out for anyone who seemed unusually interested in the agent's private life. Students also learned how to choose subagents, selecting people known by trusted contacts to be loyal and truthful yet able to keep secrets. And they learned some handy tricks like

Training involved a wide variety of activities.

Far left: Agents began their parachute training by jumping from towers like these.

Left: Two agents scale a brick wall as part of a training exercise

how to pick a lock, make a key impression with modeling clay, and write with invisible ink.

Of course, there were exams. Called schemes, they lasted 48 or 72 hours! Some tested the operative's ability to tail or lose someone in a city. The exam took place in an English city, but similar techniques could work anywhere. During other schemes, agents had to make contact with a mock resistance member, and wireless operators had to find a place in a strange city from which to transmit a message to their instructors without being detected by an unknown operative who shadowed them.

Students who were caught by the local police underwent cross-examination, a realistic rehearsal for possible Gestapo interrogation in Europe. Luckily, students unable to convince the police that their cover story was true had an escape: a secret telephone number to call for help. The SOE considered the interrogation experience so important that students who completed a scheme without being detained were sent back to get themselves arrested!

Finally, after weeks of training, an outgoing agent was ready to parachute into enemy territory.

TEACHER TURNED AGENT

Francis Cammaerts was a British schoolteacher when England declared war on Germany. He was also a conscientious objector, refusing to join the armed forces because he didn't believe in physical violence. But he changed his mind when his brother died on a Royal Air Force mission. By the end of the war, he had become one of SOE's best agents in France.

Soon after Cammaerts dropped into France in March 1943, he discovered that the Nazis had infiltrated the resistance network he had been assigned to join. He wisely set up his own resistance organization in southern France, consisting of small independent cells. If the Nazis discovered one, the others were still secure, because each cell had no knowledge of the others and so could reveal nothing if caught. Resistance members contacted him by leaving messages in mailboxes, which he sent someone else to empty. Cammaerts rarely stayed in the same home for more than three nights. He always had a well-thought-out cover story for every mission he went on, and he advised all his workers to do the same.

By summer 1944, he had organized thousands of resistance fighters, now ready to help the Allies invade southeastern France. In August, his guerrilla fighters fought the enemy to keep the road open between Cannes on the Mediterranean Sea and Grenoble in the French Alps, allowing the Allies to bypass the powerful German forces stationed further west in the lower Rhône valley.

Cammaerts was captured three days before the Allied invasion, but loyal resistance fighters freed him.

HIGH ALERT

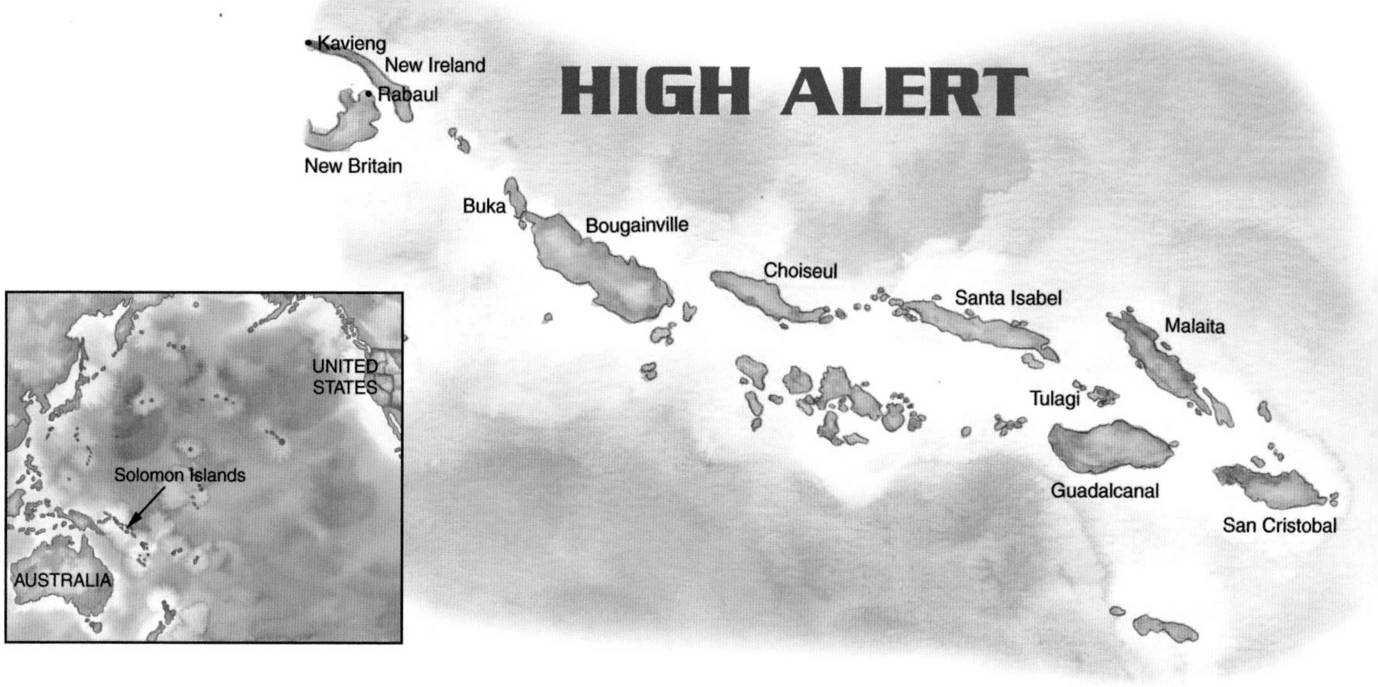
Kavieng
New Ireland
Rabaul
New Britain
Buka
Bougainville
Choiseul
Santa Isabel
Malaita
Tulagi
Guadalcanal
San Cristobal
UNITED STATES
Solomon Islands
AUSTRALIA

COASTWATCHERS

Just after the First World War (1914–18), the Royal Australian Navy realized that their nation's northern coastline could easily be invaded. Most of the area was uninhabited or sparsely populated. What's more, beyond the coast lay undefended islands with good harbors that would make perfect bases for would-be conquerors.

The Australian military decided to monitor the northern coast for unusual sightings. But the coastline was much too long for the navy to watch by themselves, so they asked civilians to help. The unpaid volunteers were called Coastwatchers. Their job was to look out for anything unusual, such as unfamiliar ships, foreign aircraft, and floating mines. Coastwatchers sent their reports to their navy contacts via telegraph. Later, the navy extended the program to Papua New Guinea and the northern Solomon Islands, both governed by Australia.

When the Second World War broke out in 1939, gaps existed in the coastwatching system. To improve it, the navy expanded the program to include non-government workers, like plantation owners. By summer 1941, there were 64 Coastwatcher stations in New Guinea and the Solomon Islands, each having a portable radio transmitter/receiver called a teleradio.

Continued on page 64

The Japanese were on a rampage. After their December 1941 bombing of the U.S. Pacific Fleet anchored in Pearl Harbor, they attacked Southeast Asia. In less than two months, they had vanquished major ports such as Hong Kong, Manila, and Singapore. Now they were headed towards Australia. Along the way, they occupied Rabaul and Kavieng, two Australian-governed islands just south of the equator, and built military bases there. Both had airstrips long enough for bombers to take off and land. This threatened New Guinea, and Australia could be next. During this mad rush, the conquerors had been decisive … and, so far, unstoppable.

South of Rabaul and Kavieng lay the Solomon Islands, a mountainous chain with hot, muggy weather suitable for growing coconuts, pineapples, and bananas. The Japanese determined that two neighboring Solomon islands—Tulagi and Guadalcanal—would work very well together as a military base. From there, the Japanese could threaten main shipping routes from the U.S. to Australia and New Zealand.

In May 1942, the Japanese occupied Tulagi, a small island with a deep, spacious harbor perfect for anchoring aircraft carriers and destroyers. Initially, they set up a seaplane base and radio station. The Allies had watched the Japanese as they advanced southward but were too busy in Europe to oppose Japan's conquests. Now, they couldn't afford to wait much longer!

The Japanese had big plans. They captured Guadalcanal, just 22 miles (35 km) from Tulagi, and began building a runway on it. Like chess pieces on a board protecting

JAPANESE ZERO

The Mitsubishi Zero was the best all-around carrier-based fighter in the early 1940s. The low-wing, single-seat monoplane was famous for its rate of climb and tight turning radius, and easily outmaneuvered Allied aircraft. But it was clumsy in high-speed dives, so Allied pilots learned to fight while diving. Also, Zeros had neither armor plate nor bulletproof glass.

A Coastwatcher uses a teleradio in the Solomon Islands

TELERADIOS

By the summer of 1942, more than 100 teleradios—newly developed voice radios—linked Coastwatchers to the Royal Australian Navy. To avoid enemy attention, Coastwatchers sent coded messages over a rarely used radio frequency.

Teleradio 3BZ had a range of about 400 miles (600 km). This was so limited that Coastwatchers had to co-operate with each other by receiving and passing on messages. The radio was made up of a transmitter and a receiver in separate metal boxes. The complete set-up, which also included a microphone, a headset, and a gasoline-powered generator, weighed 200 pounds (90 kg). It took 14 men to carry the set-up through the Solomon Islands' mountainous jungles.

In 1942, Allied fears came true when the Japanese began ravaging the southwest Pacific. Most Australian and European civilians speedily vacated the islands. In spite of the danger, many Coastwatchers remained, even though they knew the enemy would likely kill them if they were discovered. To protect the Coastwatchers as much as possible, the navy gave each one a military rank; military prisoners of war must be well treated under the rules of the Geneva Convention. (See POW Rights, page 65.) For some in particularly dangerous positions, the navy parachuted in uniforms to wear if the enemy got close. Unfortunately, the Japanese did not honor the Geneva Convention. They murdered at least 18 captured Coastwatchers regardless of rank and uniform.

Coastwatchers turned out to be much more than an early warning service. They also acted as agents behind enemy lines, keeping close watch on Japanese operations. They were good spies. After all, most of them had lived on the islands for years. They knew the land and convinced many local people to assist them. On Guadalcanal, friendly locals infiltrated Japanese camps as laborers, then told the Coastwatchers how many troops were on the island. Coastwatchers also provided shelter for downed Allied airmen.

each other, an air base guarding the Tulagi naval base would make both very difficult to attack. This posed a serious threat to the shipping route to Australia, and to the safety of Australia itself. The Allies had to act.

On August 7, 1942, American Marines and Australian forces began a dangerous operation. They planned to land troops on Guadalcanal in an attempt to take the island from the Japanese army. It was a nerve-racking move. The first troops to land would be sitting ducks for an air attack by the Japanese. Guadalcanal was well within range of the Japanese air force bases at Kavieng and Rabaul. As Allied soldiers were ferried ashore from the fleet of troopships, they kept anxious eyes on the skies, looking out for Japanese Zeros. These planes were the best all-around fighters of the time.

Fortunately, the Allies had a secret defensive weapon: a number of Australian resistance agents, called Coastwatchers, who were also watching the skies. Only four hours after the operation began, a Coastwatcher named Paul Mason radioed, "Twenty-four torpedo bombers headed yours." This warning gave the fleet time to get ready. The Allied aircraft carriers scrambled their fighters, Grumman Wildcats, into the air to wait for the Japanese attack. If they could reach a higher altitude than the enemy planes, the Allies would gain a definite advantage.

Diving at the Zeros at high speed, the Wildcats were dangerous attackers and difficult targets. Only one of the Japanese planes escaped the Allied force. The invasion of Guadalcanal could proceed.

GRUMMAN WILDCAT

At the beginning of the Second World War, the Grumman F4F—also known as the Wildcat—was the primary United States Navy and Marine Corps fighter. The single-seat, single-engine plane was rugged, reliable, and capable of withstanding a great deal of battle damage. Each Wildcat was equipped with six machine guns and two 100-pound (45 kg) bombs. Its wings could be folded (see left) when the plane was stored on an aircraft carrier, making it possible to fit more fighters on each carrier. Although the Japanese Zero was faster, the Wildcat could out-dive and out-roll the enemy.

F4F-4 Wildcat

ENGINE: 1 Pratt & Whitney R-1830-86 double-row radial engine
WINGSPAN: 38' (11.4 m)
LENGTH: 28.75' (8.9 m)
EMPTY WEIGHT: 5,785 lb. (2,965 kg)
ARMAMENT: 6 x .50-caliber Browning machine guns; 2 x 100-lb. (45 kg) bombs
MAXIMUM SPEED (at 19,800'/5,940 m & weight of 7,975 lb./3,625 kg): 320 m.p.h. (512 k.p.h.)

SCRAMBLE: *the rapid takeoff of fighter planes for action*

POW RIGHTS

The 1929 Geneva Convention protects prisoners of war (POWs), granting them such rights as shelter, clothing, food, physical exercise, freedom of religion, and correspondence.

Not everyone captured by the enemy is a POW. The 1907 Hague Convention states that a POW is a member of a military organization, which usually has an emblem that can be recognized from a distance. Members of military organizations carry weapons openly. They also follow the rules and customs of war, such as not crossing a neutral nation's boundaries.

The next day, Jack Read, another Coastwatcher, warned the fleet that a force of 45 Japanese "Val" dive-bombers was on the way. Again, Allied planes were able to intercept and destroy the attackers. Over the next five days, as the full invasion force landed, Mason and Read repeatedly saved the Allies by warning them of Japanese air assaults.

Like other resistance fighters, many Coastwatchers had unlikely backgrounds for war heroes. Some were government officials, teachers, postmasters, or managers of coconut plantations. But they didn't need to be soldiers; their job was to observe the Japanese invaders and radio information to the Allies. Many happened to have skills that were essential for this role, such as operating and repairing radios. Some had formed useful relationships with local islanders—very helpful in obtaining information about the Japanese army. Most important, they were all determined to resist the Japanese, and they all had to be brave. If the Japanese discovered their operation, the Coastwatchers could be killed immediately. Indeed, many suffered that fate.

The Japanese army on Guadalcanal was no pushover. It took the Allied invasion force six months of fierce fighting to conquer the island. During that time, the Coast-watchers continued to provide early warnings to the Allied air force of attacks by Japanese planes from Kavieng and Rabaul. The Coastwatchers' help was crucial to the successful capture of Guadalcanal.

UNDER NEW MANAGEMENT

GERMANY

POLAND

CZECHOSLOVAKIA

BELORUSSIA

Moscow •

USSR

UKRAINE

SIBERIA

Most of the Asian part of Russia is called Siberia. For centuries, Russian governments have sent enemies and criminals to Siberia's coldest and most isolated areas to work in its mining, agricultural, and manufacturing industries.

COMMUNISM VS. FASCISM

During World War II, the USSR was ruled by a repressive Communist dictatorship. This was a powerful, centralized government which believed that by the state controlling citizens' lives, all the people would ultimately be better off. Individuals couldn't own property or a business; the government exercised full control over the economy. Everyone was required to work for the state and was, at least according to theory, to be compensated based on their needs. The system never lived up to its proclaimed principles or achieved the economic standing it desired, and it was abandoned when the USSR broke up in 1991.

The governments of Germany and Italy during World War II were fascist. Fascist governments are based on the absolute authority of one party, which exercises full control over the state and doesn't tolerate opposition. They reject the Communist idea of a classless society; business is privately owned, although industry is strongly regulated by the state. Fascist states also glorify the goal of military conquest. Their ideas are highly nationalistic (they believe in the superiority of their culture over others), and consequently they exhibit strong racist tendencies.

Many Soviet citizens welcomed the June 1941 German invasion. They believed the Nazis would treat them better than their own cruel leader, Joseph Stalin. Stalin had commanded farmers to give up their land and forced business owners to hand over their operations to the government. As well, the government had deported hundreds of thousands of workers from many Soviet republics to labor camps in Siberia. (See Communism vs. Fascism, left.) Worst of all, Stalin had murdered millions of people who did not agree with his plans and ideas.

The Soviet people were correct: the German troops did treat them well … for the first few months. The invaders encouraged farmers of Belorussia, Ukraine, and other occupied republics to plant vegetables and grains. Dairy farmers, bakers, craftspeople, loggers, and others also went back to work. German leaders even attended the regions' harvest festivities.

Stalin was angry that so many Soviet citizens had accepted the German takeover. In a July radio broadcast, he reminded them that he was still their real leader and ordered them "to blow up bridges and roads, to damage telephone and telegraph lines, and to set fire to forests, stores, and transports." In other words, he expected them to fight the Germans in every possible way.

At first, most Belorussians (the people who lived in the Soviet republic just east of Poland) ignored Stalin's demands. However, some loyal Communists banded together with soldiers who had been left behind when the Red Army retreated eastward. Called partisans, these armed resistance groups hid in dense forests and wooded marshlands. Within weeks, they were joined by freedom fighters from unoccupied areas of Belorussia who sneaked through enemy lines.

Following Stalin's orders, the partisans raided German camps and supply depots. They destroyed Russian industries that provided the Germans

A partisan commander makes a phone call from his command bunker

RED ARMY: the Soviet army

ONE MAN'S SCAVENGING

Some peasants managed to acquire large amounts of abandoned Soviet weaponry. One man in the village of Dernisovka collected: 12 machine guns, 4 mortars, 160 rifles, 800 boxes of ammunition, 575 artillery shells, 489 boxes of mortar shells, 25 boxes of hand grenades, and 1,100 pounds (500 kg) of high explosives.

In addition to all of that, his 13-year-old son found: 2 machine guns, 75 boxes of ammunition, and 440 pounds (200 kg) of high explosives.

Two young partisans pose for a photograph

with grain, meat, and wood, and kidnaped local citizens working for the Germans. But they also robbed local peasants for food, clothing, and other necessities. Some village leaders trusted the Germans and asked them to protect their people from the bandits. A few Belorussians even warned the Germans about partisans hiding in nearby marshes and woods.

The peasants soon changed their minds about the Germans. By late fall, the Belorussians realized the truth: the Nazis believed they were an inferior people. The Nazis deported many able-bodied workers to German labor camps. They planned to starve the rest of the population, at the same time making them provide food and lumber for Germany.

Many peasants now rallied behind the partisans. But weapons were scarce. A few peasants discovered machine guns, ammunition, and explosives discarded by the Red Army in retreat. They also gathered weapons once used by teenagers in pre-military programs taught at secondary and vocational schools. Partisans even reused mines left in Soviet minefields the Germans had not cleared.

Later in the war, partisans captured weapons from German troops, and the Soviet government flew in ammunition and fuel, parachuting secret deliveries into temporary drop zones marked by lights. Landing cargo was even more dangerous: Soviet planes had to land on well-hidden airstrips deep in swamps and forests.

Gradually, the partisans gained control over a few areas, which they then governed like regular Soviet regions. They were connected to the rest of the Soviet Union by airplane for more than just supplies. Stalin's government was in control, directing the partisans to continuously disrupt German communication, troop movements, truck transports—and especially the railroad. The Germans transported most of their supplies on trains because Russian roads were rutted and often too muddy to travel over. This made railway bridges, stations, junctions, and tracks favorite partisan targets.

Sometimes the partisans got lucky. In the fall of 1943, one attack on a single train car yielded some unexpected, and spectacular, results. Partisans attached a remote-control magnetic mine to a tank car filled with gasoline at a Belorussian station. When the tank car blew up, the blaze ignited a nearby ammunition train, which also exploded, setting fire to an adjacent train carrying food. Finally, a fourth train, loaded with tanks, was blown to bits. As an added bonus, the explosions damaged many of the railway switches.

In another sensational attack, an exploding ammunition train set fire to a second train carrying the reserve food and medical supplies of a German division moving further into Russia.

These partisan victories taught the Germans to unload supply trains long before they reached large railway stations. Instead, trains stopped at road crossings, where soldiers transferred the goods to trucks. This tied up many German troops and vehicles, and consumed precious gasoline, but at least the Germans managed to get some supplies through.

Now the partisans began targeting roads too, choosing ones that ran through extensive, thick forests with plenty of places for the guerrillas to hide. One effective trick was to place a barrier of logs at a blind spot in the road. When a German truck came upon the logs, it had to stop and turn. The partisans then fired on the enemy. Any vehicle that managed to turn around and escape was caught by another roadblock speedily built by partisans in the direction the truck had come from.

The Germans countered by establishing a system of security points along roads leading through areas thick with partisans. Well-armed convoys of 10 to 30 trucks traveled together through the woods from one control point to the next. The Germans also encircled and slowly searched areas that concealed partisans, who were usually caught and immediately executed.

Most horrifying of all, though, the Nazis punished civilians for partisan successes, even burning entire villages and killing all the inhabitants. The German policy was to execute 10 Belorussians for every German soldier killed by partisans. Far from liberating the Belorussians from Stalin's cruelty, the Nazis subjected them to unbelievable terror.

Partisans wore whatever uniforms they could get

OPERATION BAGRATION

On June 23, 1944, the Red Army began its assault on the German Army Group Center in Belorussia, attacking its southern end with just enough troops to draw the enemy to that part of the front line. When the Germans rushed in reinforcements, the Russians launched their main attack at the northern end. The Germans then needed to move the troops they had just sent south, but partisans had destroyed all railway tracks and trains. Supply depots were demolished too.

Partisans seemed to swarm around the German troops. In fact, 143,000 partisans were operating in the vicinity of Army Group Center. They radioed German troop positions and bomb damage reports to the attacking Red Army. They cleared German minefields in advance of Soviet forces. They also provided the Russians with materials to build bridges over rivers, occupying the opposite banks until the regular forces arrived. Sometimes, after the Russian troops had crossed the river, the partisans acted as scouts and guides.

By August 1944, the Red Army had crushed Army Group Center, advancing more than 375 miles (600 km). Now they were less than 440 miles (700 km) from Berlin.

AIRCRAFT SORTIES

The Soviet air force made 109,000 flights to support the partisans, carrying 83,000 people and 16,000 tons of cargo.

WANTED: TITO

Hitler's pressure on Yugoslavia was growing ever more intense. Germany planned to invade Russia but needed to be sure that Yugoslavia would co-operate by not letting Allied troops cross its soil to attack the German rear. In March 1941, Hitler ordered Yugoslav Prince Paul to agree to Germany's terms by signing the Tripartite Pact or face an invasion. Reluctantly, Prince Paul gave in. The pact was signed on March 25. But angry Yugoslavs filled the streets of Belgrade, the nation's capital, waving placards and shouting, "Better war than the pact! Better death than slavery!"

Two days later, a group of Yugoslav military officers ousted Prince Paul. King Peter, not quite 18, assumed the throne. The deal with Hitler was off. Hitler was furious! A little more than a week later, the Germans invaded Yugoslavia. Within days, the country fell and was divided into smaller territories, each controlled by a bordering Axis nation or a local pro-German government. King Peter fled the country, eventually to London.

Yugoslav resisters took to the hills. The Germans could control Yugoslavia's urban areas but not its mountains and woods! Soldiers who had refused to surrender joined the Chetniks headed by Draza Mihailović, a colonel in the Royal Yugoslav Army. The Chetniks were loyal to King Peter. But the Chetniks had rivals, a second resistance group called the Partisans whose leader, Tito, was head of the Yugoslav Communist Party. After the war, Tito planned to replace King Peter's monarchy with a Communist government.

During the summer, both resistance groups destroyed bridges and telephone lines to isolate German troops, conducted work slowdowns at industries providing Germany with lumber and copper ore, and attacked convoys or isolated posts. But guerrilla warfare led to reprisals. The Germans threatened to murder 100 Yugoslavs for every German killed, and 50 for every German wounded. They killed men, women, and children. The smoke of burning villages covered the hills with haze.

Horrified, Mihailović decided to wait for Allied assistance to liberate Yugoslavia and restore the monarchy. But Tito refused to be bullied. The Partisans continued to fight the Germans.

The Germans covered the countryside with posters: *Wanted: Tito!* The reward—enough to make a peasant rich—was tantalizing, but not enough for anyone to turn

---

The Balkans is a group of countries in southeastern Europe that includes Albania, Bulgaria, the European part of Turkey, and the former Yugoslavia (Bosnia-Herzegovina, Croatia, Macedonia, Montenegro, Serbia, and Slovenia).

> **CHETNIK: *from the Serbo-Croat word* cheta, *"armed bands"***

THE SOUTH SLAVS

Yugoslavia was a mountainous country in the Balkans, a peninsula just south of Austria and Hungary. It was formed in 1918, at the end of the First World War. For more than two decades, a Serbian royal family ruled the nation, which was first called the Kingdom of Serbs, Croats and Slovenes. In 1929, the government changed the nation's name to Yugoslavia, which means Land of the South Slavs. In 1945, the Yugoslav government deposed the king and the nation became a republic.

Although the South Slavs had much in common, there were also many differences among them. Yugoslavia was a relatively small country (about the size of the state of Wyoming), but it had been divided many times by invading armies. For example, the Austrians controlled part of the north for more than 800 years. As a result, the north used the Roman alphabet (the alphabet North Americans use). The south and east used the Cyrillic alphabet, like the Russians. This meant that Croats and Serbs spoke the same language but wrote it differently!

Continued on page 72

Another empire (the Ottomans from Turkey) invaded the southern Balkans in the 15th century. Many Slavs who lived in that area became Muslims. But most Slavs were Christian—in the southeast and south, Eastern Orthodox; in the north and northwest, Roman Catholic. Religious differences have created many conflicts.

The Balkans is sometimes called the Powder Keg of Europe because so many wars have started in that region. The First World War began when a Bosnian Serb shot Archduke Franz Ferdinand of Austria-Hungary.

Even today, the region is in conflict. In the early 1990s, Yugoslavia began to break up into separate countries. In 2003, the name Yugoslavia was abandoned when what was left of the former nation became Serbia and Montenegro.

RECYCLED EQUIPMENT

At the beginning of the German occupation of Yugoslavia, the Partisans had to be resourceful since food, clothing, and weapons were scarce.

Other than the five-pointed red star that many Partisans placed on their hats, they wore whatever was available. Some dressed in civilian attire. Others donned recycled Italian or German uniforms with the former insignia removed. Some Partisan leaders called the German army their "uniform factory."

Dead and captured enemy soldiers also provided the Partisans with weapons. But the largest haul of all was taken just after Italy surrendered to the Allies in September 1943. Italian troops in Yugoslavia left behind tanks, anti-tank guns, rifles, and ammunition—a bonanza to the Partisans!

When the Allies shipped supplies to the Partisans, they sent weapons and ammunition they had captured from the Germans and Italians in North Africa. That way, the Partisans could continue to use any enemy weapons and ammunition they could scrounge. The Allies also provided British Sten submachine guns, which could fire Italian, German, or Allied cartridges.

Tito in. His Partisans were loyal.

News of Yugoslavian resistance trickled out to Britain. The Special Operations Executive (see page 59) promised to send the Chetniks guns and ammunition, but they offered the Partisans nothing. After all, the Chetniks represented the government-in-exile and the Partisans were Communists. Besides, Chetnik policy fit in with SOE strategy: stockpile weapons and wait for a British invasion to use them.

Then, to the SOE's surprise, the Chetniks and Partisans began fighting each other! Instead of working together to eject the Germans, both were struggling for the right to organize Yugoslavia's post-war government.

As time passed, evidence grew that some Chetniks had collaborated with the enemy. Many may have acted without Mihailović's permission, as the role the leader played is still hotly debated. Nevertheless, some Chetniks did make deals with the Germans, Italians, and pro-German Yugoslavs. They said they collaborated with the Axis to defeat Tito, sometimes even joining them in attacks against the Partisans.

Meanwhile, in November 1942, Tito organized the Anti-Fascist Council of People's Liberation of Yugoslavia (AVNOJ). The organization emphasized patriotism and played down its Communist beginnings. A year later, AVNOJ formed the National Liberation Committee, with Tito as its leader. He now controlled all of Yugoslavia the Partisans had liberated.

At about the same time, Churchill, Roosevelt, and Stalin held a conference in Tehran, Iran (November 28 to December 1, 1943), to discuss strategies to end the war. They also agreed to switch Allied support from Mihailović to Tito. The original strategy, which asked resistance groups to wait for an Allied invasion, was out of date. The Allies no longer planned to invade the Balkans, and the Partisans, who were still fighting the Axis—and finding success without Allied troops—needed supplies. It was hoped the Yugoslav Partisans (along with the Greeks) would continue to tie down 20 German divisions in the Balkans while the Allies prepared to invade France. (See Three Dots and a Dash, page 49.)

Almost immediately, the Allies dropped aid into Yugoslavia. The Allied victory in North Africa in May 1943 made it possible to send many more supplies to the

FROM PEASANT TO PRESIDENT

Tito, whose real name was Josip Broz, was born in 1892. He grew up on his father's small farm in Croatia, then part of the Austro-Hungarian Empire. At age 13, he left school to work as a metal smith, locksmith, and mechanic.

In 1913, the Austrian army drafted Tito to fight the Russians in the First World War. He was wounded in 1915, and the Russians, ruled by Czar Nicholas II, took him prisoner. After several months in hospital, the Russians sent him to a Siberian work camp. In 1917, he escaped, and a few months later he joined the Red Army during the Russian Revolution (1918–20) to help fight the czarist government that had imprisoned him. He also joined the Russian Communist Party.

Several years later, as a metal worker back home in Croatia, Tito became a prominent union organizer, fighting for workers' rights. The Yugoslav government wanted to silence him, so he used false names and identification to confuse the authorities. Finally, they jailed him from 1929 to 1934. About this time, he began calling himself Tito. The name stuck.

In 1937, Tito assumed the leadership of the Yugoslav Communist Party. The party was illegal, but Yugoslav authorities couldn't find

Tito to arrest him. He was sometimes right under their noses, on one occasion sitting quietly in a café while the police searched it. Incredibly, they did not recognize him.

Shortly after the Axis defeated and occupied Yugoslavia, Tito became leader of the Partisans. He accepted members from all ethnic backgrounds. Although many Partisans were Communists, some were not.

By 1943, Tito's army controlled many parts of Yugoslavia. After the liberation of Belgrade in November 1944, Tito and King Peter II agreed to form the nation's new government until the country could hold an election. In early 1945, Tito became premier. Of the 28 cabinet posts, 23 went to Communists. In November, the Communist-dominated government deposed King Peter and declared Yugoslavia a republic. They condemned the king for supporting the Chetniks, who the Communists claimed had collaborated with the Nazis. Now Tito was completely in charge.

Shortly after the war, Stalin began to demand absolute control over all Communist nations, including Yugoslavia. But without Russia's permission, Yugoslavia made separate economic alliances with neighboring Bulgaria and Albania. In 1948, Stalin accused

Tito of not following Communist policy. He encouraged Yugoslavs to overthrow their leader, and even set up a blockade to ruin Yugoslavia's economy. Tito turned to non-Communist nations, which responded with money and increased trade. Tito was the first Communist leader to succeed without Russian help.

By 1952, Tito began to relax his government's economic controls over its citizens. He allowed his people to open small private businesses, restaurants, and shops. The next year, the Yugoslav constitution officially allowed industry and farms to make a profit. However, Tito's secret police continued to imprison anyone who opposed him.

On April 7, 1963, Tito declared himself Yugoslavia's leader for the rest of his life. He died in 1980.

Partisans than had been sent to the Chetniks earlier. (See Recycled Equipment, page 72, and Surprise Supplies, page 74.) But Allied support did not solve all of Tito's problems: the Nazis were still looking for him. In late winter 1944, the Germans learned that Tito's headquarters was a cave hidden in the mountains of southwestern Yugoslavia. Hitler wanted the Partisan leader dead or alive.

Since the cave was only three miles (5 km) from the center of Drvar, a Partisan stronghold, the Germans decided to take the town too. At 7 a.m. on May 25, 1944, Tito's 52nd birthday, more than 300 Axis troops parachuted into Drvar. The Partisans had little time to shoot at the paratroopers as they dropped: the enemy jumped at such a low altitude that they landed in about 20 seconds! Another 300 German troops followed in gliders.

SURPRISE SUPPLIES

By the time the Allies began sending the Partisans supplies, many resistance fighters were malnourished, cold, and sick. Medical supplies were particularly valuable. Most shipments were useful, but sometimes the supplies the Partisans received from the Allies were not what they expected—or needed.

★ A shipment of an anti-malarial drug was sent—but no one in Yugoslavia had malaria.

★ A load of boots arrived—all for left feet!

★ A group of unarmed Partisans received thousands of bullets, but no guns.

★ A team of Americans working in Yugoslavia received ballots for an upcoming U.S. election. Unable to use and return the ballots in time, they put them to good use—as toilet paper.

Supplies being dropped by the RAF to Yugoslav Partisans

SECRET WEAPON

Most of the time, the Partisans had to rely on local peasants for food. Often, all the peasants had to share was ground meal patted into a ball, potatoes, or soup. Some Partisans called their spoon a secret weapon because they could use it to eat from a friendly family's pot of stew.

Draza Mihailović (center left) was the commander of the Chetniks.

The Germans had taken Drvar by surprise. The enemy split into smaller groups to capture the town, the Partisan communications center, and Allied military missions. But soon, more Partisan units arrived. When a second wave of enemy paratroopers dropped into Drvar, the Partisans met them with machine guns. They forced the Germans to retreat to the town cemetery, where a thick stone wall provided some protection.

Meanwhile, other German troops had headed for the hills to take the biggest prize of all—Tito. But they met stiff resistance: 350 determined Partisans held the enemy back. The Partisans were more heavily armed than the paratroops, and the fighting raged all day. At last, the Partisans dispersed and the Germans broke into Tito's mountain hideaway. But Tito was gone! All the Germans captured from the Partisan leader's cave was a uniform, which some say was given to Tito for his birthday.

Tito had escaped by the skin of his teeth with a small group of bodyguards. Two weeks later, he set up a new headquarters at Vis, an island 25 miles (40 km) off the Yugoslav coast in the Adriatic Sea.

A few months later, the Russians helped the Partisans clear the country of Germans. In 1946, after the war was over, Mihailović and his Chetniks faced a Yugoslav national tribunal. The government charged them with collaborating with the Axis. Most were hanged, including Mihailović.

INSIDE THE WALL

Tightening the noose! The Nazis were constantly stepping up their harassment of the Jews living in Warsaw, Poland. Six weeks after German soldiers occupied the city on September 28, 1939, the Nazis ordered Warsaw's Jews to wear white arm bands printed with a blue six-pointed star. This way, the occupying forces and their collaborators could identify them at a distance. Before long, the Jews were forbidden to ride on trains or streetcars, or leave the city without permits. They could not eat in certain restaurants or use public parks. The Nazis forced Jews to give up their businesses to non-Jews with little or no payment or compensation, and many Jews lost their jobs.

Jewish life became even more restricted after March 1940, when the Nazis declared the Jewish quarter, where most of Warsaw's Jews lived, an "infected area." The Germans claimed they wanted to protect the rest of the city from typhus, but they really planned to separate the Jews from the rest of the Polish population. The Nazis ordered all Jews to move into the "infected area" and all non-Jews to move out.

To make sure the 350,000 Jews stayed in an area normally home to 160,000 people, the Nazis forced the Jews to build a ten-foot (3 m) wall of bricks, stones, wood, and barbed wire. It was finished in mid-November 1940 and completely surrounded the quarter. Jews could not leave unless they had special permits, such as those issued to workers in German-controlled factories.

But few Jews now had jobs inside or outside the wall. To get money, they sold their furniture and other possessions. Soon, many had nothing left to sell. Most had trouble getting enough food and became sick. The Nazis issued ration cards, which limited the amount of food Jews could purchase legally—the equivalent of two potatoes or two slices of bread a day. Only the very rich could afford to buy food from smugglers, who charged high prices.

Many of the successful smugglers were children. Some crawled through holes in the wall to beg and buy food on the other side. Other children pretended to be members of large work parties in order to sneak through the gates of the ghetto. German, Polish, and Jewish police—a combination patrolled the gates—beat those they caught, or shot them dead. The Jews were terrified and, fearing even more German cruelty, did not protest.

GERMANY

POLAND

CZECHOSLOVAKIA

• Treblinka
• Warsaw

COLLABORATOR: someone who helps the enemy

ANTI-SEMITE: someone who dislikes or hates Jews

The Warsaw Ghetto

Warsaw

GHETTO: fenced-off, densely populated area where Jews were imprisoned

By 1941, conditions grew even worse as tens of thousands of Jews, evicted from neighboring towns, were herded into the ghetto. Many crammed into deserted factories and slept two, three, or more on a straw mattress. Others lived in the streets. Without facilities to wash, they were dirty and covered with lice. Many depended for their survival on watery soup from Jewish community kitchens and thin slices of rationed bread. Early every morning, funeral carts collected corpses lying in the streets. The bodies had been stripped of badly needed clothing, and were either left naked or covered with sheets of paper weighted with rocks. Bodies were buried in mass graves, without individual funerals or grave markers.

Then, on July 22, 1942, the Nazis ordered the Jewish Council (see The Judenrat, page 79) to round up an average of 6,000 Jews a day for deportation from the ghetto. The Germans said they were relocating them to labor camps east of Warsaw where they would have work and better living conditions. In fact, the Nazis packed them into cattle cars and sent them by train to Treblinka, a death camp where prison guards murdered them in chambers filled with poison gas.

The Germans lured Jews to the train station by promising—and actually giving—four pounds (2 kg) of bread and a jar of marmalade. Starving Jews accepted the offer. But after a while, the Nazis stopped offering bread. Each day, they blockaded a new area of the ghetto and searched through apartment blocks, forcing the remaining Jews out into the streets at gunpoint. Trapped Jews left their houses

German troops herd Jews out of the ghetto for deportation

The ghetto was surrounded by a 10-foot (3 m) wall. Here, three Nazis guard an opening in the ghetto wall with a machine gun.

THE HOLOCAUST

By the end of the Second World War, the Nazis had killed approximately 6 million Jews—two-thirds of the Jews living in Europe in 1939. This massacre is called the Holocaust.

Although anti-Semitism in Europe can be traced back as far as the Middle Ages, the Nazis intended to rid Europe of its Jewish population altogether. After the First World War, the Jews in Germany had become popular scapegoats for the loss of the war. Even though many Jews fought with distinction in the service of Germany, many Germans complained that Jewish businessmen had profited unfairly during the war.

Hitler used this kind of propaganda to gain political power. He blamed Jews, as well as Communists, for high unemployment and widespread hunger in Germany. Many Germans accepted

Continued on page 78

his lies. The Nazis also promoted the myth that blond, blue-eyed Germans should be the "master race." Hitler said Europe had to get rid of inferior people such as Jews, Gypsies, the disabled, and homosexuals.

Soon after Hitler was elected chancellor of Germany in 1933, his party began ordering anti-Jewish boycotts, book burnings, and discriminatory legislation. The Nazis wanted to isolate Jews from German society and drive them out of the country. The Holocaust started on November 9, 1938, with Kristallnacht—the Night of the Broken Glass— when Nazis throughout Germany and Austria destroyed synagogues and attacked Jews and Jewish-owned businesses.

After the Nazis invaded Poland in 1939, they established ghettos for Polish and western European Jews. In June 1941, the Nazis began murdering Jews in large numbers. They herded whole towns into fields to shoot them, or forced them into special vans to poison them with gas. However, the Nazis found that moving soldiers and vans from town to town was inefficient, so they built death camps, with poison gas chambers and crematoria, close to railways. Millions of Jews from across Nazi-occupied Europe were packed into cattle cars and sent for mass murder.

MOLOTOV COCKTAIL: *a bottle filled with gasoline and fitted with a wick, which explodes when ignited*

Mordechai Anielewicz, commander of the ZOB during the Warsaw ghetto uprising, died on May 8, 1943, at age 24.

and the Nazis herded them to the train station.

By the time the deportations ended in September 1942, the Nazis had killed approximately 270,000 Warsaw Jews. The Germans had sent fewer than 12,000 to work camps. Between 50,000 and 60,000 remained in Warsaw. Most worked in German factories; others hid in cellars to avoid deportation.

Many young Jews were ashamed that they had not put up more of a fight against the Nazis, hopeless though that would have been. In March 1942, three of them, Yitzhak Zuckerman, Zivia Lubetkin, and Mordechai Anielewicz, formed the Jewish Fighting Organization (in Polish, Zydowska Organizacja Bojowa, or ZOB). They united Jewish youth groups that were already active underground. It was clear to them that the Germans meant to kill everyone in the ghetto, and they wanted to die honorably—which meant to die fighting.

In January 1943, when Nazi soldiers and police entered the ghetto to begin deportations again, they were astonished to be met by armed opposition! This resistance consisted of only about a dozen fighters, led by 24-year-old Anielewicz, and was armed with only a few pistols. But it disrupted the Nazis' plans. After just four days, the Nazis halted the deportations, which boosted the ghetto's morale. The Jews smuggled more arms into the ghetto, including explosives and hand grenades.

On April 19, 1943, the Nazis entered the ghetto to deport the rest of its inhabitants. Again, the resistance surprised them. This time, the rebels consisted of 700 to 800 teenagers, members of the ZOB and a similar organization, the ZZW. These Jewish fighters even successfully attacked armored cars and a tank with Molotov cocktails. The initial German advance was quickly stopped, and a new commander, SS General Stroop, was appointed. Stroop threw more troops into the battle and changed tactics, trying to tackle Jewish strongpoints one by one. Stubborn resistance continued. The Nazis retreated after seven hours, choosing not to fight that night.

At the end of three days of fighting, the Nazis were frustrated. They decided to burn some of the ghetto buildings. This way, Jews would either die in the fire or have to flee, making it easy for the Germans to capture or kill them. Nazis began systematically burning down the ghetto on the fourth day, and continued to burn it so that by the tenth day much of the ghetto was in ruins. The Jewish fighters did not have enough weapons and ammunition to continue fighting the Germans during the day, so they retreated to bunkers, attacking German patrols at night.

By early May, the Jews were running low on food, water, and ammunition. The Germans began using dogs and sound-detecting devices to locate the resisters. On May 8, the enemy discovered the ZOB's command bunker at 18 Mila Street. When, after two hours of fighting, the Germans had failed to force their way inside, they located the bunker's ventilation points and used poison gas to try to drive the defenders out. About 15 fighters escaped, but the remaining 90 to 120 resisters—including Mordechai Anielewicz—committed suicide before the Germans broke in. No one wanted to be taken alive.

The official end to the uprising came on May 16, when General Stroop celebrated by dynamiting the Great Synagogue of Warsaw, located just outside the ghetto. He announced that the ghetto "is no more."

Two Jewish resistance fighters are captured by SS troops during the uprising

SURVIVORS

About 70 survivors of the uprising crawled through the sewer system to escape from the ghetto. Most went to the Lomianki forest near Warsaw. They were supported by some friendly Poles and Jewish underground members from Warsaw who brought them food. Over the winter, 60 of them perished, mostly from combat with anti-Semitic Poles or after capture by the Germans, and a few from exposure and illness. The remaining 10 returned to Warsaw in the spring and went into hiding. Some of them joined a group of Jewish partisans who fought under the leadership of Yitzhak Zuckerman in the Warsaw rebellion organized by non-Jewish Poles in August 1944.

THE JUDENRAT

When the Nazis forced Polish Jews into cities and then into ghettos, they required each community to form a Judenrat, which means Jewish Council in German. Each ghetto's Judenrat was responsible for governing its population and providing services such as policing and fire protection. The Judenrat distributed food and medical supplies, too. However, the Nazis also forced the councils to carry out orders, which became increasingly oppressive. The Nazis demanded that the councils provide slave laborers to work in enemy war factories and, even worse, herd Jews onto trains bound for death camps.

Some Jews thought Judenrat members were Nazi collaborators. Others believed their ghetto needed them to negotiate for better treatment. In the end, members of the Jewish Council suffered the same fate as the rest of the ghetto population: the Nazis shot or hanged them, or sent them to death camps.

DANGER AHEAD

"**T**he supreme battle has begun …" French general Charles de Gaulle announced in a radio message to the people of France. It was 6 p.m. on June 6, 1944—D-Day. Waves of American, British, and Canadian troops had already landed on the beaches of Normandy. (See Operation Overlord, page 38.) De Gaulle, leader of the Free French forces (see The Free French, page 82), proclaimed that at last it was time for the French to force the Nazis out of their country.

An all-out effort would be the key. After the Nazis had occupied France in June 1940, hundreds of independent resistance groups had emerged one by one. However, they had often disagreed about how and when to combat the enemy. The Armée Secrète (AS), the resistance that supported de Gaulle, had been watching for the general's signal. Until now, de Gaulle had told them to fight only if they had to. Groups supported by the Special Operations Executive (see page 59) in London had also remained quiet. They were waiting for the Allied invasion. On the other hand, the Communist Francs-Tireurs et Partisans (FTP) had fought the Germans any way they could from late 1942 onward, even though many of their assaults had been ineffective and the Nazis retaliated by punishing and killing civilians.

Now that the Allies were on French soil, all resistance groups dropped what they were doing to spread the word. Excited yet fearful, they dug out the guns and ammunition they had hidden in their homes, barns, and churches.

Meanwhile, news of the Normandy invasion reached Das Reich, Germany's 2nd SS Panzer Division, stationed 450 miles (720 km) south of Normandy. Das Reich had been in the Montauban area since late April, waiting for orders in the event of an Allied invasion. The 15,000-strong division could provide crucial reinforcements for the defense of the coast.

About 2,500 of Das Reich's troops were veterans just returned from the eastern front, but most of the division consisted of inexperienced 17- and 18-year-old raw recruits. The D-Day invasion meant that the new troops, who had been training in the countryside, would see their first action. The waiting soldiers filled vehicles with fuel, checked their artillery, and assembled their guns and ammunition.

SOE-trained Tony Brooks was also preparing for Das Reich's move. He wanted the German departure to be as

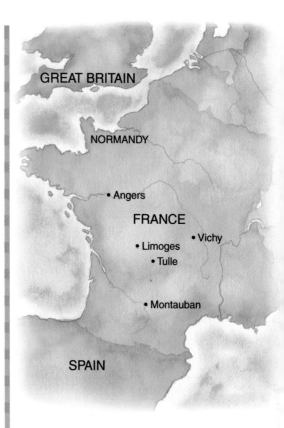

VICHY FRANCE

After a short but dramatic campaign, the French surrendered to the Germans on June 22, 1940. As part of the surrender terms, the Germans occupied more than half of France—the north, including Paris and the Atlantic and English Channel coasts. Southeastern France, including the Mediterranean coast, remained under French control. The capital was the spa town of Vichy. The leader was Marshal Philippe Pétain, a First World War hero, who largely co-operated with the Nazis.

SABOTAGE: to damage or destroy something in order to hinder the enemy

SABOTEUR: someone who commits sabotage

An American officer and a member of the French resistance during street fighting in France

THE FREE FRENCH

When Germany occupied France in June 1940, General Charles de Gaulle, a little-known army officer and junior government minister, did not accept defeat. Instead, he fled to London and immediately tried to rally the French behind him. On June 18, over BBC radio, he urged his countrymen to join him in England and fight for Free France.

Free French forces grew slowly: by the end of July, only 7,000 volunteers had joined him. But two years later, de Gaulle had organized a small but effective military force that fought in North Africa and Italy. The 2nd Free French Armored Division participated in the later stages of the Battle of Normandy.

When the Allies drove the Germans out of France, de Gaulle formed France's provisional (temporary) government and served as its president. By 1945, the French First Army contained eight divisions, which participated in the Allies' final offensive into Germany.

STEN GUN: British submachine gun, with an accurate range of only about 50 feet (15 m)

chaotic as possible. The longer Das Reich was delayed, the more time Allied troops would have to gain a foothold in Normandy.

Brooks realized that the Germans would move their armored tanks to the coast on railway flatcars —faster and less damaging to the vehicles than traveling by road. So he and his band of freedom fighters, who worked for the French national railway, "fixed" most of the available flatcars. Pretending to be doing routine maintenance, the saboteurs injected an abrasive paste, supplied by SOE in London, onto the flatcars' axle bearings. The paste would cause the axles to seize up after a few miles of travel. Other teams replaced the connectors on electric trains with burnt-out ones. Still others blew up railway tracks with plastic explosives.

When the Germans discovered that the flatbed cars were breaking down, they were horrified. Now Das Reich's troops and vehicles would have to travel most of the way to Normandy by road. So, at dawn on June 8, long rows of tanks, half-tracks, and trucks lined up to leave Montauban—more than 1,400 vehicles with 110 yards (100 m) between each in case of air attack. At first, the vehicles and 15,000 men moved easily through open country, where resistance fighters had no place to hide. Nevertheless, the tanks were not built for traveling long distances over roads. Within a few miles of Montauban, the steel pins that connected the tanks' track segments began to break. Maintenance crews had to repair or replace them. Brooks's gamble to destroy the railway flatcars had paid off. Constant repairs to the tracks would definitely slow Das Reich down!

At 8:30 a.m., Das Reich met its first resistance. They were Maquis, men who had been hiding in the hills to avoid being sent to Germany to work in factories. Many Maquis had joined de Gaulle's AS or the Communist FTP. Now, a small band of about 15 Maquis crouched around a bridge at the north end of a village and opened fire on Das Reich's lead infantry units. The German vehicles halted and troops jumped out, taking cover among the village's buildings and trees. Slowly, they worked their way around to outflank the Maquis at the bridge. Along the way, the Germans killed five townspeople, then shot five Maquis before the others fled into the woods. The skirmish had delayed the German trek towards Normandy by an hour, and time was precious.

As Das Reich progressed northward during the rest of the morning and afternoon, more Maquis ambushed the Germans. They also built roadblocks of felled trees and wagons along the route. Although Das Reich's heavy vehicles easily swept the roadblocks aside, the resistance did bog the enemy down for another three hours.

The next morning (June 9), a Scottish member of a Jedburgh team learned that parts of Das Reich's armored column—half-tracks, tanks, and trucks—were traveling north towards the town of Tulle. Major Tommy MacPherson and his team had parachuted into France the night before. Leaving his two Jedburgh partners in camp to avoid jeopardizing their lives too, MacPherson and 27 Maquis headed for a small bridge along Das Reich's route.

MacPherson told two Maquis to wrap the barrels of their Sten guns in wet towels to make them sound like machine guns when fired. After rigging the bridge with explosives, MacPherson and 10 Maquis waited nearby while the others hid in the woods. As the German division's lead half-track crossed the bridge, a Maquis detonated the charges. The bridge burst into flames. Another Maquis tossed a Gammon grenade that ruptured a tank's track. The road was blocked! Forced to stop their vehicles, German troops worked their way forward on foot, taking cover among the trees. Das Reich's trained soldiers killed 20 of the 27 inexperienced Maquis. But the fighting had delayed the division for another couple of hours.

By June 10, broken-down tanks and artillery littered the roads from Montauban to Limoges. The Germans had traveled only about one-third of the distance to Normandy

Hitler and members of the paramilitary SA, or Sturmabteilung, which is German for "Storm Troops." The SS began as a branch of the SA, gaining its independence in 1934.

SCHUTZSTAFFEL

SS is short for Schutzstaffel, which is German for "protective squad." Originally Hitler's personal guards, by 1933 the SS had evolved into an elite corps. Members of the SS were so blindly devoted to Nazi goals that they would do almost anything to achieve them—forcing foreigners into slave labor, trying to Germanize citizens of conquered territories, and murdering Jews, Gypsies, and Communists in concentration camps.

Always separate from the regular German armed forces, the SS grew rapidly, as did the number of its roles. In addition to armed divisions that fought alongside the German army, the SS took control of German intelligence, the Gestapo (secret police), concentration camps, and the day-to-day policing of conquered populations.

ORADOUR-SUR-GLANE

German troops on their way to fight the Normandy invasion attacked Oradour-sur-Glane, a village 14 miles (22 km) from Limoges, on June 10, 1944. Why the Germans chose the small town is still a mystery. Some say a German officer planned to avenge the death of a friend. Others say Oradour-sur-Glane was a den of Maquis.

On that sunny Saturday afternoon, German soldiers fanned out through the town firing shots into the air. They ordered all citizens to assemble at the fairground near the town's center, claiming they wanted to check everyone's identity papers. Young and old moved quickly; they did not want to anger the Germans. Once the townspeople reached the fairground, the soldiers separated the men from the women and children, supposedly to simplify the identity check.

Suddenly, the charade was over. The soldiers forced the men into garages and barns. A few minutes later, the Germans began shooting the Frenchmen, then covered them with hay and brush and set the buildings afire.

Meanwhile, other soldiers locked the women and children inside a church. Then soldiers carried a large box into the building, set it down, and lit a fuse. Women and children screamed as black smoke poured out of the box. The Germans fired their guns and tossed grenades. Later they heaped straw and chairs on the dead, and set the church on fire. In no time, the entire building and everyone in it were ablaze.

The soldiers burned the rest of the town that evening. Only a few men, women, and children escaped to tell the rest of the world what had happened. German soldiers had murdered 648 civilians.

GAMMON GRENADE: homemade hand bomb made by wrapping fabric around an explosive charge, then sewing on a fuse that exploded on sharp contact

Each Jedburgh team consisted of three men (one each from Britain, the U.S., and the country they were sent to). They were dropped behind enemy lines to support resistance fighters who needed training.

but already needed spare parts for more than half of their tanks and one-third of their towing vehicles and half-tracks. While maintenance crews stayed behind to get the damaged vehicles running, troops up ahead had to stop and wait for the rear to catch up.

Finally, on June 15, Das Reich's armored vehicles boarded a train to Angers, a town still 100 miles (160 km) from Normandy. Now closer to the action, the armored vehicles moved only at night to avoid being bombed by Allied aircraft. Meanwhile, the non-armored units continued by road.

During the second half of June, Das Reich trickled into Normandy, reaching the battlefield in dribs and drabs until June 30. Each resistance group had done its part to delay the German division's progress towards Normandy. Many lives were lost, but not in vain. Das Reich's trek should have taken three days. Instead, it took two to three weeks—valuable time for the Allies to establish their positions in France before they pushed the Nazis back into Germany to defeat them.

MIXED RECEPTION

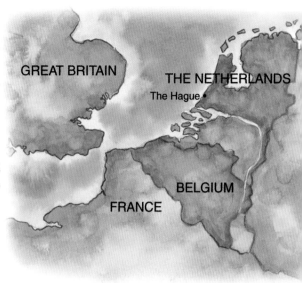

The Netherlands didn't stand a chance. In less than a week in May 1940, the Germans overpowered Holland's small army and air force. The Dutch were taken by surprise, having believed that Germany would respect their country's neutrality. Although the Nazis claimed they would treat the Dutch fairly, before long they deported thousands of Dutch laborers to Germany to work for their war industries. Even worse, the Nazis began persecuting Dutch Jews, eventually sending all they could find to concentration camps, where more than 100,000 died. Holland's future looked grim.

Meanwhile, the British government had formed an organization it believed would help free the Netherlands. In 1941, the Special Operations Executive, better known as the SOE (see page 59), began to parachute agents into the Netherlands to assist the freedom fighters there. Unfortunately, the Abwehr was lying in wait. Hermann J. Giskes, a talented spymaster, was Hitler's chief of counterespionage in Holland.

Giskes had skill and experience behind him, but in late 1941 he almost missed a lucky break that seemed too good to be true. A member of his staff had recruited a diamond smuggler to spread false information to a fledgling Dutch resistance movement. Giskes refused to accept the smuggler's tales that the underground organization had been sending messages to England. In fact, his response was, "Go to the North Pole with your stories." Giskes didn't believe him because the German police hadn't detected any illegal radio transmissions.

The smuggler was telling the truth. Soon, the German police did detect an illegal transmitter. Using direction finders, they narrowed the sender's location to a single block in a suburb of The Hague. Next, they pinpointed the building, then followed the signal to an apartment inside. They'd found it!

The police raided the apartment of radio operator Hubertus Lauwers in March 1942. Before the police entered the building, Lauwers escaped and ran down the block, but a member of the Abwehr saw him. The police captured Lauwers a few blocks from his apartment with, would you believe, three coded messages in his pocket. Sloppy work: he should have destroyed them. As it turned out, Lauwers was the radio operator for the group the smuggler had ratted on, an SOE cell. His radio had gone

THE NETHERLANDS

The Netherlands is often called Holland. The people who live there call themselves Hollanders or Nederlanders, but people in English-speaking countries call them the Dutch.

> **THE HAGUE: *a Dutch city on the Netherlands' southwest coast***

DIRECTION-FINDING TEAMS

German direction-finding (D/F) teams were numerous and competent. Their job was to find illegal radios used by members of the resistance. If the operator's radio was plugged into an electrical current, a transmission from a large town that lasted more than half an hour was sure to bring a detection van to the door. The Germans established what part of a town an operator was working in simply by turning off the city's electricity district by district. When the transmission was interrupted, they knew where to start looking. The Germans narrowed the search by driving a D/F van through the streets, and then on foot, holding miniature listening sets to their ears.

Naturally, secret agents preferred to transmit from small towns where there were fewer German police, but that was not always possible. At times,

Continued on page 87

undetected before because it had been broken.

Giskes promised Lauwers he would spare his life if he agreed to transmit messages to London. Confidently, Lauwers did as he was told. He knew that the SOE would spot his pre-arranged secret warning signal. His security check was to make a deliberate mistake every sixteenth letter. If captured, he was to send messages with no mistakes. Lauwers convinced the Germans that his security check was to misspell the word *stop*.

Unfortunately, no one in London noticed the absence of the agreed security check. Instead, SOE radioed back that a new agent was about to parachute in. Giskes was pleased. He sent a welcoming committee—Abwehr agents posing as Dutch resistance fighters. The impostors cleverly disarmed the newcomer, telling him that if German patrols searched them, they would be arrested for carrying firearms. They also told the SOE agent that London had mixed up some messages, so they would need more information about his identity and mission. To the SOE agent, the meeting appeared normal until after the reception committee was satisfied that it had garnered enough information. Then the welcome was over and the committee arrested him.

Giskes realized that the radio link to London would lead to the capture of more SOE agents, as well as radio equipment, guns, and ammunition. With a sense of humor, he christened the operation North Pole (or Nordpol in German). Now he was a believer.

Messages continued back and forth between the Netherlands and England, and Giskes kept sending reception committees to pick up new agents. Three times, Lauwers sent hints to London, mixing *CAU* and *GHT* into the gibberish that preceded and followed each cipher message. But SOE kept missing the signal.

Within a few weeks, Lauwers's entire resistance cell was captured, but Giskes was too nervous to enjoy his success. He was afraid other SOE cells operating in the Netherlands would discover that he and his radio operators were pretending to be SOE agents over Lauwers's radio. Giskes feared that one day an SOE drop would be a bomb instead of another agent.

agents needed to transmit important information before they could get to the countryside. To power their transceivers, some used batteries, which, unfortunately, had to be constantly recharged. A trick was to change the crystal frequently during each message, thus altering the radio's frequency. Another was to transmit from different locations. But the safest practice of all was to keep messages brief.

DIARY OF A YOUNG GIRL

Anne Frank was a German-born Jew who moved with her family to the Netherlands in 1933, when she was four, the same year the Nazis came to power. Her happy childhood was interrupted a month before she turned 11, when the Germans invaded Holland. Two years later, the Nazis began deporting Dutch Jews to "work camps"—really death camps. Anne's parents hid in some rooms above her father's business. They were in hiding for more than two years. To pass the time, Anne wrote in her diary.

Two months after Anne's fifteenth birthday, someone informed the Nazis about the Franks' secret home. In August 1944, the Nazis raided the hiding place and deported the family to death camps. Seven months later, Anne died of typhus.

But Anne lives on through her diary. The family friend who had saved it for Anne gave it to her father, the only member of the family to survive the Holocaust (see page 77). He had it published in 1947. Today, kids around the world can read *Anne Frank: Diary of a Young Girl*, published in 67 languages.

SUITCASE RADIOS

Most SOE radio operators used a short-wave Morse code transceiver—a transmitter and receiver combined. The B Mark II was the type generally used. It weighed 32 pounds (15 kg) and fit into a 24-inch (60 cm) suitcase. Operators used two or more removable crystals (pieces of quartz) to change their radio's frequency. One was used during the day, the other at night. Crystals were small enough to hide in the palm of a hand, but easily broken and difficult to disguise. Even harder to conceal was the 70-foot (21 m) aerial, which needed to be spread out during transmissions.

FOLLOWING ORDERS

Sometimes, Giskes and his staff were forced to carry out SOE orders. If they didn't, London would know the Abwehr controlled the SOE radios in Holland.

One SOE message told the resistance to blow up and sink a thousand-ton barge. Reluctantly, the Abwehr complied. The harbormaster's motorboat stood by to rescue the crew.

Another message received by the Abwehr requested the resistance to send agent Jambroes to England. The Germans stalled for as long as they could with excuses, eventually reporting that Jambroes had disappeared in a police raid. In his stead, they agreed to send Jambroes's deputy. Of course, they didn't send the real deputy but an Abwehr officer in disguise, who traveled with a genuine agent. In a "surprise" raid before they left German-occupied Europe, the phony deputy was "captured." But the real agent was allowed to escape to London to tell the SOE that the Nazis had arrested Jambroes's deputy. The story sounded legitimate, keeping the SOE from discovering the truth that Giskes's agents had been sending and receiving Jambroes's messages.

The Abwehr occasionally refused to oblige an SOE request. When the resistance was told to assassinate local collaborators, the Germans replied that they couldn't because they needed telescopic sights for their rifles. What a relief for the Abwehr: the rifle sights never arrived!

Meanwhile, SOE in London hadn't a clue that anything was wrong. By mid-spring 1943, they believed the Dutch resistance was ready for action. In reality, the Abwehr controlled more than a dozen SOE radio channels and had executed most of the 50 or so agents SOE had dropped in, plus a few who had already been in place.

Finally, the British received a break! Two SOE prisoners escaped from their German captors and reached England in late fall 1943. They told SOE that Giskes had been controlling Dutch SOE operations for more than a year, but at first the British refused to believe them. Apparently, nobody had noticed Lauwers's hidden messages. What's more, no one had questioned why all the airdrops had been in Holland's south. Someone should have known that drops in the south would have to go through numerous German checkpoints before arriving at their intended destination in the north.

Realizing that Operation North Pole had probably been discovered, Giskes signed off with this message to London on April Fool's Day 1944:

We understand that you have been endeavoring for some time to do business in Holland without our assistance. We regret this the more since we have acted for so long as your sole representatives in this country, to our mutual satisfaction. Nevertheless we can assure you that, should you be thinking of paying us a visit on the Continent on any extensive scale, we shall give your emissaries the same attention as we have hitherto, and a similarly warm welcome. Hoping to see you.

THE OSLO GANG

Gunnar Sonsteby was on the Nazis' most-wanted list in 1944. Norway's Nasjonal Samling government was pro-German, but Sonsteby was a Norwegian resistance leader struggling to drive the Nazis out of his country. Germany had invaded Norway in April 1940 to stop the British from shutting down shipments of Swedish iron ore sent to Germany through a Norwegian port. Norway's King Haakon VII fled to London to set up a government-in-exile. Many patriotic Norwegians also went to England, and some attended schools run by the Special Operations Executive (see Prep School, page 59). Like Sonsteby, they returned to Norway to fight with the resistance, known as the Home Front.

By 1944, the Germans wanted Sonsteby for committing sabotage in and around Oslo, Norway's capital. The pro-Nazi state police were also looking for 10 of Sonsteby's cohorts. But the Oslo Gang, as the freedom fighters were known, were hard to find. The gang would meet for a few hours to steal Nazi documents or spring someone from jail, then they would disperse and fade into the Norwegian population.

The Oslo Gang's secret was that many Norwegians were helping them. Workers at an auto body shop regularly repainted the gang's five vehicles and replaced their phony license plates. Resistance supporters working for state agencies like the Department of Roads and Highways supplied the gang with false permits, which helped them pretend to be working on ordinary jobs if the state police stopped them.

The gang even knew an executive in the petroleum industry who agreed to hide 100,000 gallons (440,000 l) of gasoline for them. Gasoline was scarce and reserved for Nazi vehicles. Civilian cars and trucks had to have gas generators mounted on them to convert burning wood, charcoal, or anthracite coal into a gas to power the engine. Tar from the burning fuel tended to clog the air coolers and engines if a vehicle idled for long periods. The Oslo Gang needed fast, reliable cars and trucks on their missions, and that meant using gasoline. But to look like they were obeying the law, the gang mounted gas generators on their vehicles.

The Oslo Gang had another trick up their sleeve: forged identity papers. The Nazis made everyone in occupied Europe carry papers with information such as the bearer's name, age, and address. Nazi authorities could demand to see them at any time. Anyone without papers was arrested. Since the Nazis were looking for the Oslo Gang, members often assumed false identities and carried phony papers. Most of

NAZI INVASION OF NORWAY

The Nazis invaded Norway on April 9, 1940, simultaneously attacking its six main seaports, including Oslo, the capital. The Allies landed troops at Trondheim and Narvik, two cities on the western coast, but they were forced to retreat in early June. King Haakon VII and some of the Norwegian government escaped to London.

The Germans appointed a puppet government called the Nasjonal Samling, led by Vidkun Quisling. Much like a puppeteer manipulating the strings on a marionette, the Nazis controlled the Norwegian government. After the Nazis surrendered on May 8, 1945, Quisling was convicted of treason and shot. *Quisling* is now an international word meaning "traitor."

King Haakon VII returned to Norway on June 7, 1945.

the gang had papers that said they worked for the state police. Even better, they had state police contacts, too—spies who warned the gang of police raids, suggested how and when to break someone out of jail, and advised them which officers could be trusted. Their tips kept the Oslo Gang one step ahead of the Nazis.

In May 1944, someone informed the Home Front that the Nasjonal Samling was about to send Norwegian males between the ages of 21 and 23 to fight the Russians on the eastern front. (See Eastern Front, page 23.) Soon, the government would order this age group to report for Labor Service duty, but instead of assigning them to work on farms or build roads, it would make them join the army. Most eligible Norwegians were anti-Nazi and unwilling to fight a war for Hitler's cause, so they boycotted the registration.

However, the Nasjonal Samling had another way to locate the young men who qualified: a punch-card machine used to sort government data on Norwegian citizens. It was a kind of primitive computer that separated perforated cards according to where holes were punched. One hole might indicate that a citizen was male, another that he was born in 1922, and a third that he lived in Oslo. Using the machine, the government could collect the addresses of all males of the right age, then pick the young men up one by one.

The Home Front contacted the Oslo Gang, who sneaked into a Nasjonal Samling office building and blew up the machine. They also destroyed the only other compatible machine in Norway, owned by an insurance company.

The Nazis would have to find the young men another way, so they conducted street sweeps. Police stopped any male who looked 21 years old and asked to see his papers. Anyone who did not hand over his papers was jailed until he could prove who he was. To escape the street sweeps, young Norwegian men fled to the forested countryside to live in makeshift camps.

To force the young men out of their hiding places, the government changed the way it handed out ration cards. Until then, the government had given ration cards to the heads of families, but now it planned to give them to individuals. Everyone in each family had to appear in person to receive their cards … including the hiding men. Without ration cards, most would starve to death, but if they showed up for their cards, the Nazis would nab them!

Printing fake ration cards for the fugitives was not an option for the Home Front since no one, including SOE in

The Oslo Gang after the German surrender in 1945

SEIZING THE EVIDENCE

In April 1945, when the war was almost over, the Norwegian Nazis began to burn their archives, destroying evidence of their reign of terror. But the Home Front wanted to salvage documents kept by the Nazi police and Nazi Department of Justice that contained the names of collaborators and informers. The Home Front asked the Oslo Gang to help them steal the files.

Fortunately, Gunnar Sonsteby, the gang's leader, had a trusted police contact who posted the guards at the gate into the courtyard behind the police and justice buildings. The contact found two willing, though extremely nervous, guards.

At 6 p.m., Sonsteby entered the Department of Justice building with four other men, two of them dressed as police. Most employees had already left for the evening, but the Oslo Gang found the caretaker and a few others still working. The gang told the workers they were searching for dangerous resistance propaganda hidden in offices. While two members of the gang guarded the caretaker and the other employees, a department secretary in on the plot showed Sonsteby around. The secretary

Continued on page 92

unlocked doors and pointed out which files contained the most important information. The gang members began to pile files in the corridors.

At 6:30 p.m., the courtyard guards let a van with *Oslo Express* on the sides through the gate. The rest of the gang jumped out of the van and entered the Nazi police building. The building's caretaker, an accomplice, maintained the switchboard during the robbery. The gang stole two tons of documents and a safe weighing more than 1,500 pounds (700 kg). The safe was too heavy to carry, so they rolled it down the stairs. The gang quickly loaded the van with another 1,000 pounds (450 kg) of files from the Department of Justice, then sped out the courtyard gate. But they were not safe yet! A few blocks away, they made a quick stop to remove the van's name boards—the police would be looking for a van marked *Oslo Express*.

The Nazis had already burned numerous files, but the Oslo Gang saved many important documents used to convict collaborators and informers at trials after the war.

RATIONING

Ration cards were slips of paper that shoppers handed to clerks with their money when they purchased such items as food and tobacco. Resources in wartime were scarce, and rationing was a way to make sure that no family bought more than the government allowed. Below is an American ration coupon for sugar, which quickly became a luxury. People now had to line up to purchase it.

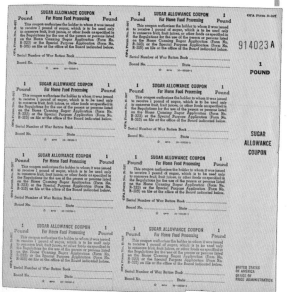

England, could find the right kind of paper. So the Home Front decided to steal real ration cards from the plant that printed them. Since the plant was located in Oslo, they called in the Oslo Gang.

The plant was guarded, but the gang knew that a delivery truck filled with ration cards was scheduled to leave the building at 8:30 a.m. on August 9, 1944. Perfect timing was important. As the printer's truck neared the first intersection, the Oslo Gang's gray Ford approached the same intersection from the right. The gang's car had the right of way, so the printer's truck had to stop. This was their chance! Sonsteby and two men, armed with pistols, jumped into the truck's cab. Quickly, they drove off to transfer the booty to a resistance vehicle. In all, the gang captured 70,000 ration books, 30,000 supplementary cards, and 30,000 tobacco cards!

The gang helped two of the printer's men escape to Sweden in case the police believed they had helped the robbers. But the other two delivery men wanted to stay in Norway, probably to remain with their families. The gang tied them to the truck so they could tell authorities they had been overpowered.

Next, the Home Front notified the Nasjonal Samling that the resistance had captured the cards. They offered the Nazis a deal: the Home Front promised to return the cards if the Nasjonal Samling would repeal the command for everyone to appear in person for their ration cards.

No deal! Five days after the heist, government-controlled newspapers reported the theft and offered a reward for any information leading to the gang's capture. The articles also announced that the Nazis were punishing everyone for the theft: they canceled five days' worth of tobacco and alcohol rations.

No one came forward to claim the reward. Finally, the Nasjonal Samling gave in, reversing the order for citizens to appear in person for ration cards. The Home Front returned most of the stolen cards but held back 13,000 to feed resistance members on the Nazi hit list. Home Front members on the run could not risk showing their identity papers to get ration cards. Although their papers could often fool the police, under close scrutiny the Nazis would be sure to discover they were bogus.

Best of all, the Nazis finally gave up the idea of sending young Norwegians to the eastern front.

PHOTO CREDITS

3 upper right, Official U.S. Navy Photograph, 80-G-16511 **32 upper,** Rear Admiral John D. Bulkeley, USN, NH54383 **65,** National Archives, 80-G-66154. All courtesy U.S. Naval Historical Center
3 lower right, Courtesy USAMHI Special Collections Branch: www.carlisle.army.mil/cgi-bin/usamhi/pixdata/presentpix.pl?pic=/Low-Resolution/scenes/ww2/armorshp.jpg
3 left, NWDNS-226-FPL-MH (23) OSS, Field Photographic Branch **13,** NWDNS-226-FPL-2665(A) OSS, Field Photographic Branch **22,** NWDNS-111-SC-193903 Spangle, Department of Defense. Department of the Army. Office of the Chief Signal Officer **27 left,** NLR-PHOCO-A-48223659(48) **37 upper left, back cover right,** NWDNW-44-PA-660 Jack Betts, OEM. OWI. DOB. BSS **38 upper, back cover middle,** NWDNS-26-G-2343 Department of Transportation, U.S. Coast Guard, Office of Public and International Affairs **48,** NWDNS-208-PU-138LL-3 OEM. OWI Overseas Operations Branch **50,** NWDNS-80-G-331330 Messerlin **61 right,** NWDNS-226-FPL-MH(126) OSS, Field Photographic Branch **77 left,** NWDNS-238-NT-282 Office of the U.S. Chief of Counsel for the Prosecution of Axis Criminality **82,** NWDNS-111-SC-217401 Department of Defense. Department of the Army. Office of the Chief Signal Officer **84,** NWDNS-226-FPL-T(25) OSS, Field Photographic Branch. All courtesy NARA
6, MacLean, U.S. War Dept., Adjutant General's Office—Monthly catalog 1942, p. 140 **7,** OWI Monthly catalog 1943, p. 94 **17,** Milton Arthur Caniff, United States. Office of Civilian Defense **92,** Office of Price Administration. All courtesy Northwestern University Library www.library.northwestern.edu/govpub/collections/wwii-posters/
8, USHMM, courtesy of Hans Aussen **57 lower,** USHMM, courtesy of David Diamant Erlich **57 upper,** USHMM, courtesy of Benjamin (Miedzyrzecki) Meed **68 upper, back cover left,** USHMM, courtesy of Museum of the Great Patriotic War **69,** USHMM, courtesy of Eliezer Zilberis **74 right,** USHMM, courtesy of Muzej Revolucije Narodnosti Jugoslavije **77 right,** USHMM, courtesy of National Archives **78,** USHMM, courtesy of Yad Vashem Photo Archives **79,** USHMM, courtesy of National Archives **83,** USHMM, Heinrich Hoffmann/Studio of H. Hoffmann, courtesy of James Sanders
9, Australian War Memorial Negative Number 024677 **15,** Australian War Memorial Negative Number PO2127.004 **16,** Australian War Memorial Negative Number 020684 **21,** Australian War Memorial Negative Number 025155 **32,** Australian War Memorial Negative Number 116360 **33,** Australian War Memorial Negative Number P01339.004 **38 lower,** Australian War Memorial Negative Number 128302 **40,** Australian War Memorial Negative Number PO2018.223 **47,** Australian War Memorial Negative Number 128342 **56,** C. H. Isaac. Australian War Memorial Negative Number UK2808 **61 left,** Sutton. Australian War Memorial Negative Number 133741 **64,** H. A. Mackenzie. Australian War Memorial Negative Number 306814 **74 left,** Australian War Memorial Negative Number SUK13565
12, Lt. Brin, Signal Corps Photo, NARA MM-Bri-7-28-43-R2-6 Compiled by CPT John F. Curley, courtesy of CMH Online
20, Special thanks to Bletchley Park: www.bletchleypark.org.uk
25, 26 left, 26 right, 27 right, All courtesy The Funet Russian Archive
28, Sammelwerk Nr. 15, Gruppe 66, Bild Nr. 184. 1923. LOT 3633 Reproduction Number: LC-USZ62-12667 **44,** U.S. Army Signal Corps. Reproduction Number: LC-USZ62-25122. All courtesy Library of Congress/Famous People
35, 37 right, middle left, lower left, Special thanks to Hans Moonen, of Airdropped and shelled propaganda leaflets of World War 2: http://members.home.nl/ww2propaganda/
43, Special thanks to Bonnie Henning, Research Analyst, and The Institute of Heraldry: www.perscom.army.mil/tagd/tioh/tioh.htm
52 upper, Alfred T. Palmer. OWI. Overseas Picture Division. LC-USE6-D-004935 **52 lower,** U.S. Army Signal Corps. OWI. Overseas Picture Division LC-USW33-000389-ZC DLC. All courtesy Library of Congress/Prints and Photographs
53, Special thanks to Dennis Schneider of ww2surplus.com: www.ww2surplus.com/
60, Special thanks to Lynn Philip Hodgson, Author, *Inside Camp-X*
68 lower, 87, Courtesy Yad Vashem Archive
73, Courtesy AP/Wide World Photos
88, 91, Courtesy Norway's Resistance Museum

GLOSSARY

ABWEHR: the German military intelligence service and espionage organization

ALLIES: the alliance during the Second World War that included Great Britain, France, Australia, Canada, India, New Zealand, South Africa, the United States, and many other nations

AMPHIBIOUS LANDING: an operation in which ship-borne troops land on an enemy-held coast

ANTI-SEMITE: someone who hates or dislikes Jews

AXIS: the alliance during the Second World War that included Germany, Italy, Japan, Finland, Hungary, Bulgaria, and Romania

BATTALION: an army unit of roughly 500 to 1,000 men, usually divided into three companies

BEACHHEAD: the land taken on an enemy's shore, captured to protect future landings of soldiers and supplies

BRIGADE: an army unit of roughly 3,000 to 7,000 men, usually divided into three battalions

COLLABORATOR: someone who helps the enemy

D-DAY: the Allied invasion of Normandy on June 6, 1944, that led to the liberation of France and the invasion of Germany

DIVISION: an army unit of roughly 10,000 to 20,000 men, including all sorts of support staff, and usually divided into three brigades

FRONT: a line of battle on which advance or defense is based

GESTAPO: Nazi secret police

GHETTO: fenced-off, densely populated area where Jews were imprisoned

GREAT BRITAIN: England, Scotland, and Wales

NAZI: a member of the National Socialist German Workers' Party. Nazis believed in a strong centralized government headed by a leader with absolute power.

NEUTRAL: a country not at war

PANZER: the short form of the German word for *tank, panzerkampfwagen,* which means "armored fighting vehicle"

PARAMILITARY: civilian group that acts like a military organization

PARATROOPER: a soldier trained and equipped to jump from an aircraft with a parachute into a battle area

PROPAGANDA: a campaign designed to either help or damage a cause by affecting minds and emotions

RECONNAISSANCE: a look at something to gain information

SABOTAGE: to damage or destroy something in order to hinder the enemy

SABOTEUR: someone who commits sabotage

SOE: (Special Operations Executive) the British agency responsible for sabotage, resistance, and other sorts of unconventional warfare in Axis-controlled territory

UNIT: a group of soldiers who live, train, and fight together. Units can range in size from four men to more than 100,000.

UNITED KINGDOM (U.K.): the shortened name for the United Kingdom of Great Britain and Northern Ireland, made up of England, Scotland, Wales, and Northern Ireland

Italicized numbers denote illustrations and definitions.

INDEX

ACKNOWLEDGMENTS

Many thanks to:
Tina Forrester, for making these stories as energetic and vivid as they could be.
David Craig, whose illustrations continually amazed, as always.
Sheryl Shapiro, who worked untold hours on this project and juggled multiple roles.
Laura Ellis, for her excellent advice and comments.
Sandra Booth, the sleuth who hunted down so many of the photographs found in this book.
John Sweet with his eagle eye, and the staff at Annick Press, for their support.
Special thanks must go to Lieutenant-Colonel John Marteinson and David Kaufman, for their suggestions and corrections. Of course, any errors and omissions remain mine alone.
—Stephen Shapiro

Sincere thanks to everyone who helped make this book possible, but especially:
To Stephen Shapiro, whose enormous wealth of knowledge includes myriad Second World War stories.
To creative director Sheryl Shapiro, who worked long hours to fit the text, artwork, and photos into 96 pages.
To David Craig, whose artwork entices readers to delve into the text.
To researcher Sandra Booth, who searched long hours to find just the right photos ... then had to search again when we had to make changes.
—Tina Forrester

The publisher would like to thank Lieutenant-Colonel John Marteinson, Editor of the *Canadian Military Journal*, for reviewing the manuscript and providing invaluable feedback and suggestions.

The publisher would also like to thank David Kaufman, director of the recent documentary *From Despair to Defiance: The Warsaw Ghetto Uprising*, for reviewing the story "Inside the Wall" and providing important insights and helpful comments.

Special thanks also to Ivar Kraglund, of Norges Hjemmefrontmuseum, Hans Moonen, Bonnie Henning, Dennis Schneider, Lynn Philip Hodgson, the staff of Bletchley Park, and the anonymous Timaham for both their images and their patience. Additionally, Dr. Ronald Haycock, RMC, and the staff of the Ghetto Fighters' Archive were both kind and helpful in their referrals.

BIOGRAPHIES

Stephen Shapiro (Toronto) is a lifelong aficionado of military history and has spent many years studying the strategies and operations of the Second World War. He is the co-author of *Ultra Hush-hush* (also with Tina Forrester) and a recipient of the Canadian War Museum History Award.

Tina Forrester (Toronto) is both a writer and researcher on a broad spectrum of subjects. Her previous works include *Create Your Own Millennium Time Capsule*, *The Birthday Book*, and *Ultra Hush-hush* (with Stephen Shapiro).

David Craig (Toronto) is an illustrator renowned for his depictions of historical settings, events, and people. Along with *Ultra Hush-hush*, his previous works include the dramatic illustrations in *A Day That Changed America: Gettysburg*, *Attack on Pearl Harbor*, and *First to Fly: How Wilbur and Orville Wright Invented the Airplane*, which won the 2003 James Madison Book Award.

To all those who lost their lives in what was more than just a test of wits.
—S.S.

For Tom, who often eats late and postpones holidays to support my love of research and writing.
—T.F.

To my mentor and high school teacher, John Topelko.
—D.C.